The Walls of Rome

Archaeological Sites
General Editor: Malcolm Todd
Reader in Roman Archaeology,
University of Nottingham

Already published
Hengistbury Head
Barry Cunliffe

The Walls of Rome

Malcolm Todd
Reader in Roman Archaeology
University of Nottingham

Paul Elek London

First published in Great Britain in 1978 by
Elek Books Ltd
54–58 Caledonian Road, London N1 9RN

ISBN 0 236 40126 2 (cased)
ISBN   0 236 40108 4 (paper)

Printed in Great Britain by
The Camelot Press Ltd, Southampton

Contents

Figures

The fall of Empires? What can that mean? Empires, being neither up nor down, do not fall. They change their appearance, and it is people who speak of overthrow and ruin: words which hide the whole game of error and deception. It would be more correct to speak of *phases* of Empire.

Galliani

Preface

The late Roman walls which surround the city of Rome are among the most impressive monuments of that city and form perhaps the most complete and complex work of fortification surviving from the ancient world. Perhaps because of its very size, the city wall was for long neglected by students. It was not until 1930 that the first, and to date the only, complete study of the wall and its associated works, that of I. A. Richmond, was published, and by that time much had been lost to the ravages of man and climate. Richmond's outstanding book, *The City Wall of Imperial Rome*, thus appeared at an opportune time. The destructive agencies were largely held in check, access was possible to most of the structure, and general scholarly interest in Roman fortifications was on the increase. The sensitive and meticulous treatment which Richmond accorded to his subject makes the book one of that scholar's most admirable achievements of observation and record. Any subsequent account of the wall and its structural history, and indeed of late Roman fortification, is bound to lean heavily upon Richmond's work.

For two main reasons a fresh account of the wall of Rome seems necessary. First, since 1930 much has been learnt about other late Roman fortifications, especially in the western provinces, so that we are now in a better position to set the Aurelianic work, and its later accretions, in its proper context. Secondly, Richmond's book is now a rarity, not to be found even in all specialist libraries. This short account of the wall of Rome is thus offered to a new generation of students and visitors who may wonder about the significance of these great works which frown above the hurtling traffic of modern Rome.

1

The origins of Rome and the first defences

From the lower valley of the river Tiber to the promontory of Circeii 80 km away to the south there stretches a belt of open coastal plain. Rising through this plain some 25 to 35 km from the sea are a number of volcanic hills, the highest—Mons Albanus to the Romans—reaching to about 1,000 m. To the north the valleys of the Tiber and Anio offered open country for settlement and cultivation. To the south the plain was restricted by the projection of Mons Lepinus, jutting out from the Apennines towards the sea, and by the Pomptine marshes, not drained until the first century A.D. This small and not very distinguished plain was Latium, the cradle of Rome and her empire.

The land was fertile but its working presented certain difficulties to its early settlers. The plain was covered by a rich alluvial clay, lightly mantled by volcanic dust. The many springs and water-courses had greatly assisted the formation of a humus layer well suited to the growing of arable crops. But flood-water rushing down from the Apennines in spring and autumn could not pass through the underlying dense clay, so that low-lying ground tended to become waterlogged and to require intensive drainage. There were also problems of communication. The Apennines to the east effectively cut off Latium from the rest of the peninsula. Even communication along the coastal plain towards the bay of Naples was made difficult by the spur of Mons Lepinus and the Pomptine marshes at its foot. On the northern front, along the Tiber, matters were a little easier, but even here the river, though by no means impassable, did not have many natural crossing points. Thus the local geography marked out Latium as a distinct and unified block of territory, well suited to agricultural settlement and protected by nature from the depredations of all but the most determined of neighbours.

From at least 800 B.C., settlers began to exploit the farmlands of Latium, making especially for the Alban hills in the centre. Particularly favoured situations for the earlier villages were the steep-sided but not elevated spurs which projected into the plain from the east. At one point, the river Tiber had broken through a ring of low volcanic hills rising 30 m above the plain. On the east bank of the river an arc of four spurs obtruded into the narrow, marshy valley and within the encircling ring of higher ground lay three small hills. This was to be the site of Rome.

Archaeological investigation over the past half century has provided us with an increasingly clear picture of the earliest settlements on the hills of

Rome.[1] Controversy does indeed still surround the dating of the early phases of settlement and the origins of the first settlers, but we now possess substantial material evidence where once there was only the legend of a foundation from Troy, the native tradition of Romulus and Remus, and the foundation date of 753 B.C. which probably did not enter the canon of Roman thought on this subject until the first century B.C.

Latium appears to have been only sparsely populated in earlier prehistoric times. During the second millennium B.C., the Bronze Age Apennine culture had permeated the plain and the volcanic hills, and the presence of Apennine culture pottery on the site of the later Forum Boarium suggests the existence of a homestead or small village on one of the near-by hills about 1500 B.C. But the earliest firm evidence for permanent settlement on the hills of Rome relates to the eighth century. Small communities of farmers and stockmen then existed on the hills of the Palatine, Esquiline and Quirinal, and perhaps also on the Caelian. On the valley floors and on the slopes lay the interments of their dead. By the mid seventh century, these little communities had grown large enough to send some of their members to colonize the land on the valley floor. Before 600 B.C. the marshy area later occupied by the Roman forum had been drained and settled. The only buildings so far known to belong to this phase are small timber huts framed upon a small number of upright poles, the walls being no more than screens of wattle and daub, and the roof a thatching over a framework of small branches. Public buildings such as temples are not in evidence from this early time.

Change in peasant communities such as these usually comes very slowly, and so it was with Rome. During the seventh century, the inhabitants of three or four distinct communities appear to have drawn closer together.[2] Their pottery and metalwork became more uniform and is found in all the villages. Differences of wealth, and thus presumably of prestige, became apparent and this phenomenon may well be connected with the growing evidence of contacts with areas outside Latium. About 625, Etruscan *bucchero* pottery and metal objects appear in Rome, brought in most probably from the nearby Etruscan towns of Veii and Caere. More elaborate houses shortly began to appear, often still timber-framed but now including brick structures provided with tiled roofs. There is little doubt that these advances were due to the import of Etruscan ideas and technology as well as objects. Traders from Veii only 12 km away to the north may well have played their part, but successful Etruscan diplomacy or warfare must also be suspected, for now the Roman literary tradition accords with the findings of archaeology and reports that in the late seventh century B.C. the Etruscan king Tarquinius Priscus became king of Rome. The separate hill-villages had steadily drawn together, by the natural growth of communities which found themselves in favourable environments, by the sharing of religious festivals and cults, and by the apparent need to combine against powerful neighbours, especially to the north of Latium. The survival of Rome in this changed world was assured by her position, but it seems unlikely that she could have long held out against Etruscan expansion southwards. Probably shortly before 600 B.C. Rome became a vassal of Etruria.

Etruscan expertise in architecture and engineering transformed Rome. Several major streets which were to survive until Imperial times (among them the Sacred Way) were now laid out. Public buildings which were the artistic equals of those in older Etruscan centres were built in the sixth and fifth centuries, the best attested being a temple of Vesta on the Sacred Way dating from 575–50 and a group of shrines in the Forum Boarium. The Capitoline hill was now brought into the city and it seems to have been intended to serve as the main religious focus, a large and richly appointed temple of Jupiter being built on its southern side. The growing wealth of Rome and the artistic ambitions of her richer inhabitants are evident in the fine terracotta antefixes and friezes which once adorned the temples, in finds of superb metalwork in bronze, and in imports of high quality Greek painted pottery.[3] The city-state had come of age and entered its first phase of prosperity.

The earliest defences

According to later traditions, the first defences of Rome were erected during the phase of Etruscan domination. The second king of Rome, Servius Tullius, the son-in-law of Tarquinius Priscus, who ruled from 578 to 535 according to the traditional chronology, was believed by later Romans to have constructed a massive stone wall around the city. The historian Livy,[4] writing in the late first century B.C., reports that the project had been planned by Tarquinius Priscus but was eventually carried out by his successor. Livy, like other writers of the early Empire, believed that the wall of Servius Tullius could be identified with a massive stone *enceinte* which could still be seen in his day encircling the Capitol, Palatine, Caelian, Quirinal, Viminal, Aventine and part of the Esquiline (fig. 1). By the late first century B.C. this great wall had long been out of use, appeared to be of great antiquity, and could thus be identified with the only early defences of the city mentioned in the historical tradition. But Livy and his fellow historians were mistaken. Although the wall of Servius Tullius alone was mentioned in the annalistic records, it was not the only or the earliest defensive work built around Rome. Further, as we will see later, the great stone wall dated from a time long after Servius.

Before the massive stone circuit traditionally attributed to Servius was built, an earlier defensive work, consisting of a massive earth *agger* or rampart with a broad ditch outside it (fig. 2), had surrounded parts at least of the city. This work is best known from its surviving course across the plateau east of the

Quirinal, Viminal and Esquiline.[5] In this sector it is followed by the later 'Servian' wall. Elsewhere, its course has been incompletely traced and it may not have formed a complete circuit around the city, but perhaps existed in discontinuous lengths which were designed to cover areas vulnerable to attack or raiding. The known length, for example, cuts off an enemy's approach to the centre of the city by way of the narrow valleys between the Quirinal and Viminal, and between the Viminal and Esquiline.

A small number of cuttings have been dug through this huge rampart.[6] A section of the 'Servian' wall still extant in the garden of the old Italian Ministry of Agriculture was shown to have an earth rampart lying behind it. The earliest levels in the rampart had been cut away at the front to insert the wall, and the bank was later heightened by more layers of earth, probably immediately after the wall was constructed. The earlier phase of the earthwork contained a sherd from an Attic red-figured *kylix*, a drinking-cup, which dates from the early years of the fifth century B.C. The date of the first rampart should thus be no earlier than about 480 B.C., and probably no later than about 450, unless the Greek sherd came to be in the rampart as a result of a still later intrusion. Another section across the earth rampart, made during the building of Rome's main railway station in 1861, confirmed that there were two phases of construction, an earthwork preceding the massive stone wall, without adding any details as to the absolute dating of either work.

The first known defences of Rome, then, dated not from the reign of her second king, but from the first half of the fifth century B.C. They were earthwork defences, probably resembling the still visible earthworks at Ardea, thought to date from the same period, and they may not have provided complete protection of the city. Were there defences earlier than this earthwork? It is not impossible that the growing city of the sixth century was protected by more than its natural defences alone, but as yet no evidence of any defensive work has been recovered. The villages of pre-regal Rome may have been individually enclosed by timber palisades or simple bank-and-ditch defences, like many other Iron Age settlements in most parts of Europe, but even this is not certain. Much remains to be done in the field, when opportunity allows, before the full story can emerge.

The fifth century was a period in which Rome's military strength received its first trials. By a blend of diplomacy, constant border-raids and counter-raids, and outright aggression, the position of Rome as the acknowledged mistress of Latium was confirmed by 493. The peoples living in the hill-country to the east presented greater problems, and it was not until the end of the century that the most formidable of these, the Volsci, had been pushed out of the coastal plain. But the greatest Roman success was the defeat and destruction of the rival city of Veii, 12 km away to the north, after long periods of raiding. It took a ten-year siege (406–396) before this powerfully

THE 'SERVIAN' DEFENCES

Fig. 1 General plan of the 'Servian' wall.

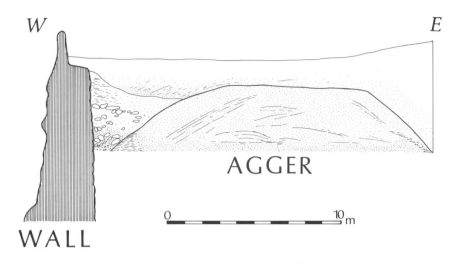

Fig. 2 Section across 'Servian' wall and earlier rampart, east of the Viminal near Piazza dei Cinquecento.

defended fortress-town, as large as Rome and better protected by nature, could be taken and utterly destroyed. Veii rose again but was thereafter never more than a prosperous country town. The spoils of war were great. Rome acquired a considerable amount of loot and almost doubled her subject territory. But very soon Rome herself was to experience a catastrophe almost as complete.

North and west of the Alps lay the warlike tribes of the Celts. At some unknown date within the fifth century, Celtic bands began to cross the Alps and settle in the north Italian plain. They shortly began to attack Etruscan cities and succeeded in taking some by storm. In 391, an army of Celts burst deep into Etruria and in the following years aimed at Rome. In 386 their host penetrated to the river Allia only 15 km from Rome before they were confronted by Roman levies. The Roman forces were swept aside by the invaders and their city lay wide open. The Celts were slow to move forward but when they did they found no obstacles in their way. Rome was easily captured and the subsequent devastation was extensive. Its debris has now been revealed by excavation on several sites on the Palatine and in the Forum. The defenders managed to hold out on the Capitoline for seven months having improvised elementary defences on the summit, but in due course were starved into submission. The Celtic army, which had come so far south for loot rather than territory, accepted a ransom in gold and promptly departed. The building of Rome could begin again, almost anew, and with one significant addition to the plan.

The 'Servian' wall

During the great work of nineteenth-century clearance which preceded the building of modern Rome, many stretches of a massive fortification (fig. 3) lying well within the circuit of Aurelian's Wall were brought to light.[7] There seemed at that time no reason to doubt that this was the wall to which Livy referred as being constructed by king Servius Tullius late in the sixth century B.C. and which by Livy's own day no longer served as a work of defence, being difficult even to discern in places. The name 'Servian' was therefore given to this wall, following the usage of this term in Imperial times, a name which it still retains having acquired a virtually inalienable right to stand. From an early time during the disinterment of the wall, difficulties surrounding the traditional dating were apparent. The remains were by no means homogeneous in character and constructional detail. Two quite distinct building stones had been employed, the one a grey, volcanic tufa known as *Capellaccio*, the other a yellowish tufa of better quality, the so-called *Grotta Oscura*. *Grotta Oscura* came from quarries near Veii which, as we saw earlier, came into Roman possession no earlier than the early fourth century B.C., so that it cannot possibly have been used in Rome over a century before in the time of Servius Tullius. A difficulty of equal magnitude is raised by the ambitious scale of the work. So powerful was it that even Hannibal in 211 B.C. felt that to invest it would be fruitless. It is hard to accept that the population of Rome in the late sixth century B.C. would have been numerous enough to construct and man this circuit, which measured 10 km in length. It would have been an impressive achievement even for the Rome of a much later time.

There is now widespread agreement that the 'Servian' wall was built shortly after the Gaulish sack of the city about 386, this dating providing both a credible historical context and a satisfactory explanation for the presence of *Grotta Oscura* in the fabric. Unfortunately there has been little archaeological investigation along the line of the wall of a kind likely to produce precise and reliable dating evidence. But nothing has yet been recovered to invalidate a dating to the early fourth century B.C.

The intention of the builders of the huge new fortification was to give to the city a unity denied it by its topography. Its course may now be traced, starting from the Capitol, where earthwork defences may have been hastily improvised during the Gaulish siege. The small eminences of the Capitol and the Arx were surrounded on their western flanks and the wall, turning sharply eastwards, was pierced by a gate at the foot of the Arx, and then made for the Collis Latiaris and Collis Mucialis, passing thence along the northern edge of the Quirinal. In this sector the wall held to the top of the escarpment, resulting in many sharp-angled turns and re-entrants. Close to the point where the Via Nomentana entered the city, the wall swung sharply to the south and for

Fig. 3 'Servian' wall near the railway station. (Fototeca Unione)

much of the eastern side of the *enceinte* ran in fairly straight lengths to cover the Viminal, Cispian and Esquiline heights, here following in part the early fifth-century defences. An abrupt eastward turn then carried the wall up the slope of the Caelian hill before it turned westwards once more, clinging to the southern edge of the hill between the Via Tusculana and the Via Appia. A large salient brought in the hill south-east of the Aventine, the wall then curving around the south and west faces of the Aventine and running straight on to the west edge of the Palatine. Another straight length linked the Palatine with the Capitol thus completing the circuit.

For much of its course this massive wall was terraced into the hillsides it surrounds, and on the eastern side of the circuit, as we have already observed, it revetted the earlier earth rampart. Such terraced walls are also known at Ardea, dating probably from the late fourth century B.C., and at the third-century town of Falerii Novi. In the best preserved sectors, the 'Servian' wall measures some 3·6 m wide at the base, and the accompanying ditch 29·6 m wide and 9 m deep. A flat berm of about 7 m lay between wall and ditch. The character of the masonry is massive and in places almost Cyclopean. The individual blocks of tufa vary in length from 75 cm to nearly 2·1 m, in width from 45 to 66 cm. On average they measure some 60 cm in height. The courses were arranged alternately in headers and stretchers. No projecting towers were provided either at the time of the original fortification or later. The gate-openings seem to have been simple: the single carriageways were covered by towers placed against the internal wall face, a gate-type which persisted until the first century B.C. in Italy.

There were later modifications to the 'Servian' wall. In 87 B.C. the consuls faced by the army of Gaius Marius tried to strengthen the city defences by digging new ditches, restoring the wall and making emplacements on it for

Fig. 4 Emplacement for a catapult, inserted in the 'Servian' wall in 87 B.C. (Mansell Collection)

catapults. A well-preserved example of one of these emplacements, an arched opening piercing the wall, can still be seen on the Aventine (fig. 4). The subsequent history of the wall is unknown in detail but it was presumably one of progressive decay and dilapidation. There is no record of it again being called on to serve as a line of defence for the city, although part of the circuit was unsuccessfully used by the emperor Vitellius in A.D. 69 in a desperate effort to keep the Flavian army out of Rome. Nor was the 'Servian' wall yet replaced by another circuit. During the period when the empire of Rome reached the summit of its power, the *Urbs* itself had no effective defences.

2
The Aurelianic defences

Aurelian, *Restitutor Orbis*[8]

In the middle decades of the third century the Roman Empire passed through the most perilous time in its history. Within, ambitious soldiers with no claim to rule other than the armies at their backs competed with each other for the now tarnished dignity of the Imperial purple. Beyond the frontiers, to the north especially, the weakness of Rome did not pass unnoticed. New groupings of peoples were emerging, most of them powerful confederacies forged from numerous small tribes: Franks, Alamanni, Saxons, Goths. In the east the old Parthian enemy, long held in check by skilful diplomacy and limited campaigning, now saw his chance. Nor was that all. Grave economic ills afflicted the life of the provincials. Inflation was virtually out of control and the currency issued by the mint was increasingly debased and worthless. The Empire might well have fallen apart at this time: indeed it began to do so. Gaul, the German provinces, Britain and parts of Spain were drawn away from the central Empire by Postumus in A.D. 260 and his *Imperium Galliarum* was maintained for the next fourteen years. The city-kingdom of Palmyra, situated in an oasis in the Syrian desert half-way between the Mediterranean and the Euphrates, and grown rich on the dues it levied on the caravans which passed through it, fell into the hands first of Odenathus, nominally an agent of the Roman emperor, and later (in 268) of his widow Zenobia, whose ambitions were wider than those of her husband. For a time, most of the eastern provinces were effectively under her direction.

Thus when Lucius Domitius Aurelianus was proclaimed emperor in 270, following the death of Claudius II (generally known as Claudius Gothicus) of the plague, it is difficult to think of less auspicious circumstances for an accession. In his brief reign of four years, Aurelian tackled all the major problems confronting the Empire and achieved successes beyond all reasonable expectations where many had failed before.

Like many of the soldier-emperors of the third century, Aurelian was of humble birth, originating from the Balkan provinces, perhaps from Sirmium in Pannonia. His long years of military training (he was fifty-five when he was hailed emperor) had imbued him with the ideals of an army which was still, despite increasingly formidable enemies, a proud and powerful fighting force. His nickname *manu ad ferrum*—'hand on hilt'—had evidently been well earned. A man of immense stamina and strength, this determined, disciplined and industrious soldier lacked none of the military virtues dear to the old

Roman order. In matters of diplomacy and high politics he was less well equipped, being somewhat inflexible and unsophisticated. But that he was far from inhuman is clear from his generous treatment of former opponents. In the desperate times in which he came to power, and given the prevailing *mores* of the day, not the least surprising aspect of Aurelian's reign is the upright character of the emperor himself.

The exigencies of the day meant that he was quickly into action. The Danube frontier had been pierced by Juthungi and Vandals, and shortly afterwards the Juthungi broke through again and this time reached Italy and began to threaten cities there. The threat was quickly dealt with and the remnants of the barbarian host made their way northwards after suffering crushing defeats. In the following year, 271, Aurelian decided upon a major alteration to the Danube frontier. The province of Dacia, which lay north of the river in what is now western Romania, acquired by Trajan's campaigns in the early second century, was given up and its army and administrative personnel withdrawn. A new province of Dacia was created on the south bank of the Danube, carved out from territory formerly included in Moesia and Thrace.

Aurelian was clearly conscious that the Danube frontier was crucial to the defence of Italy and thus of Rome. Once an enemy had eluded or broken through the Danube garrisons, there was little in the way of military forces between him and the heart of the Empire. On several occasions in the preceding century barbarians had penetrated northern Italy, but had always been distracted by rich prizes there from attacking Rome. But it was becoming increasingly obvious that it would only be a matter of time before a strong invading force plunged deep into the peninsula. Not only would they find that there were relatively few Roman troops to oppose them. They would also discover, if they did not already know, that Rome had no walls.

The city was therefore now surrounded by a massive new circuit of defences, measuring in all 18 km in length (fig. 5). Though the work began in 271, it was to take about a decade to complete in its first form. There were to be many subsequent modifications and rebuilds, particularly to the towers and gates, but the Aurelianic defences were to remain the principal shield of Rome throughout the rest of the Empire and indeed retained in part a military function down to the nineteenth century.

Aurelian's wall: the first phase

The course adopted by the builders of the wall naturally brought much more ground within the defensive circuit than the 'Servian' wall had done. The total area now enclosed was more than double that surrounded by the fourth-century circuit, all fourteen of the Augustan regions being included. At no

AURELIAN'S WALL

P. SALARIA

P. PINCIANA
P. NOMENTANA

CASTRA
PRAETORIA

P. CHIUSA

1. PORTA FLAMINIA
2. PORTA PORTUENSIS
3. PORTA AURELIA
4. PORTA SEPTIMIANA
5. MAUSOLEUM OF HADRIAN (CASTEL ST. ANGELO)

ESQUILINE

P. TIBURTINA

P. PRAENESTINA

CAELIAN

AMPHITHEATRUM CASTRENSE

P. ASINARIA

P. METROBIA

SERVIAN WALL
ROADS
AQUEDUCTS
P   POSTERN

P. LATINA

P. OSTIENSIS EAST

P. ARDEATINA

P. APPIA

0   1   2
km

Fig. 5 General plan of Aurelian's wall.

point did the new wall follow the course of the old, though near the Porta
Metrobia on the south-east side the two circuits are less than fifty metres apart.
Aurelian's wall does, however, appear to follow an earlier boundary, at least
on the north and south sides of the city. This was a customs or toll boundary
which existed certainly since the first century A.D. and which was marked out
by boundary stones in the late second. Apart from its enclosure of the most
important areas of the city, the course of the wall was clearly dictated by the
needs of defensive strategy. Hence there are two major salients in its line, one

Fig. 6 The wall and towers between Porta Appia and Porta Ardeatina. (Fototeca Unione)

on the south side where the Appian Way came in after crossing the valley of the Almo, the other west of the Tiber, where part of the hill of the Janiculum overlooking the island and its bridges was brought within the fortifications. The wall itself measures nearly 4 m in thickness and still survives in numerous places to a height of 20 m (fig. 6). Originally there were eighteen gates, of which nine still remain, and several posterns and smaller openings of which six are certainly recorded. At an interval of about 30 m towers projected from the wall, 381 in all. On the western side long and low walls ran along the Tiber bank, linking the Trastevere salient with the main fortified area. Only one bridge was left outside the fortifications, Pons Aelius, and this was covered by a bridgehead fort thrown round the great brick drum of the Mausoleum of Hadrian. The constructional technique evident in the wall fabric is simple. The

Fig. 7 Blocked arcades of the *Ampitheatrum Castrense*. (Fototeca Unione)

Fig. 8 Remains of an apartment house embedded in the wall in Via di Porta Labicana. (Fototeca Unione)

core is an aggregate of tufa held in a cement made from lime and pozzolana sand. The facing is of thin tiles or bricks mortared together. Only in the structure of certain of the gates was stone employed.

Although the new defences were sited close to the limits of the city, it was inevitable that buildings of various kinds would lie in their path. There were many of these, including a fort, an amphitheatre, houses, aqueducts, boundary walls and a considerable number of tombs, particularly close to the principal roads. The fort was the *Castra Praetoria*,[9] the base of the Praetorian Guard, which retained its military function after the building of the wall. Likewise, the *Amphitheatrum Castrense*, built in the early third century, continued to function but now had its southern arcades closed up by the wall builders (fig. 7). Many structures, however, were already of great antiquity by 271, had gone out of use by then, or had their use terminated by the arrival of the wall. Several houses and at least one tenement-block were adapted without ceremony to fit into the defensive structure. For instance, near the north-west angle of the *Castra Praetoria* a large house, or what remains of it, can still be seen embedded in the wall fabric (fig. 8). Its vaults had been filled with rubble and the wall built right through the rooms. Any projecting walls or other features were simply shorn away. Again, near the modern Porta San Lorenzo, a garden wall with statues still occupying its niches was bodily incorporated in the core of the new defences.

The structures most commonly damaged by the wall or embodied in its fabric were tomb monuments. The most striking case is the famous pyramid of Gaius Cestius (fig. 9). Several large monuments happened to lie close to

Fig. 9 Pyramid of Gaius Cestius, with wall and Porta Ostiensis East in the background. (Mansell Collection)

main roads on sites chosen for gates by the wall builders. Not infrequently, the larger tombs were utilized as part of the core of the massive gate-towers, any awkward or unnecessary protuberances being trimmed away. Thus, the great tomb of Vergilius Eurysaces was put to a new use in the central tower of the Porta Praenestina. At the Porta Salaria, two monuments were buried in the eastern tower, while the western was founded on the tomb of Cornelia Vatiena. There were many others. In all, Richmond calculated that earlier structures accounted for about one-tenth of the total circuit, i.e. 1·8 km. Homo's estimate was that as much as one-sixth of the *enceinte* was so composed, but this seems too high.[10]

Apart from any intrinsic interest these earlier structures may possess, they perform a vital archaeological function, that of providing an absolutely secure *terminus post quem* for the building of the wall. This may not seem to be of outstanding significance since the literary tradition attributes the inception of the defences to the early years of Aurelian's reign. But the literary sources for the middle and later third century are far from impeccable. Indeed the principal source for Aurelian's reign is the all too peccable *Historia Augusta*, now held by some historians[11] to be an outright forgery of the late fourth century. The written tradition, therefore, needs confirmation from any possible quarter and this is effectively provided by the battered and despoiled buildings and monuments immured in the defences.

Many of the incorporated structures were, of course, of a respectable antiquity before the wall was planned and can therefore have no real bearing on its date. The cumulative evidence from buildings in use until a much later date is decisively in favour of a construction date after, and most probably well after, the early decades of the third century. For example, certain of the rooms in the Lateran palace were occupied—and twice modified—before they were broken into by the building of the wall.[12] Since these rooms were themselves not constructed before about A.D. 200 the wall can hardly have been built before the middle of the century at the earliest. Another early third-century building, a garden house inside the *Horti Spei Veteris*, was cut off from its associated mansion by the wall, and this too cannot have occurred before about 250. The wall covering the salient west of the Tiber also cut through houses occupied in the early and mid third century. From both sides of the Tiber, then, this kind of evidence demonstrates that the wall was built not long after the middle of the third century, but was in existence before 300, as the total absence of late third-century remains in deposits antedating the wall makes clear. The written tradition is thus vindicated as fully as it can be by the available archaeological evidence, short of a massive programme of excavation.

The overall composition and design of the wall is the product of two major phases of construction, and within each phase different treatment was

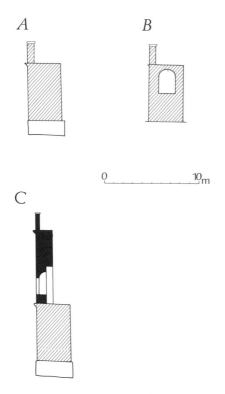

Fig. 10 Sections across the wall:
A Aurelian's wall of the solid type
B Aurelian's galleried wall
C Aurelian's wall with Maxentius' gallery above

accorded to different parts of the circuit. Above the foundations there rose a solid structure, 4 m thick and 6·5 m high, of brick- or tile-faced concrete (fig. 10A). Large numbers of the tiles had clearly been taken over from older buildings, as considerable numbers of the stamps on them date from the reign of Hadrian. On this wall stood a continuous gallery, some 8 m high on average and having a thick wall to the front and an open arcade to the rear. Over this gallery there was a rampart-walk, originally protected by now vanished merlons at the wall front. Narrow slit-windows or loop-holes set at varying intervals in the front wall of the gallery complete the defensive scheme. Later modifications, rebuildings and repairs can be distinguished at many points but around the entire circuit these two principal phases of construction are normally in evidence and they plainly were responsible for the greater part of the fabric of the wall.

The earlier, solid wall was built as a complete work in itself, as is

Fig. 11 Early twentieth-century view of Aurelianic galleried wall with Maxentian gallery above. The wall front has fallen away. Viale Castrense, between *Amphitheatrum Castrense* and Porta Asinaria. (Fototeca Unione)

demonstrated by the fact that it possessed a parapet and merlons. In many places these can still be seen embedded in the brickwork of the later wall. The lower wall thus formed an independent entity for a period before the gallery was added above. In certain sectors, however, the wall of the first phase itself included a gallery (fig. 10B).[13] Between Porta Asinaria and the *Amphitheatrum Castrense*, the wall was solidly built only to a height of 3 m and above that point there stood a low, barrel-vaulted gallery supporting the rampart-walk and the parapet (fig. 11). Similar structural variations seem to have existed near Porta Pinciana and at Porta Metrobia. This striking anticipation, on a smaller scale, of the later type of wall in these limited sectors can most probably be explained with reference to the personnel responsible for building (below p. 43).

The structure of the wall, of whatever type, was simple and strong. The foundations were laid in a trench 4 m wide, revetted by wooden shuttering which was in many sectors left in position as the concrete hardened. On sloping or irregular ground the footings were sometimes stepped, faced with tiles or blocks of tufa and left exposed above ground. In this way the top of the foundation was maintained at a fairly uniform level. The wall, 3·6 m thick, rose upon this solid base, the slight narrowing being achieved by one or more offsets. It appears from the evidence of the visible building-joints that the wall was built in sections measuring 4·5 to 6 m in length, 1·3 to 1·8 m in height and extending right through the thickness.[14] The joins have almost invariably been carefully finished off and are not always easy to identify. No putlog-holes are evident so that the builders must have worked from the wall top as the work proceeded, or perhaps from freestanding scaffolding. The facing was uniformly of tiles, each one broken to a triangular shape and embedded in the concrete with its smooth side outwards. The core, consisting of a concrete aggregate, was packed in tightly behind the facing. Horizontal stability was given by courses of large tiles occurring at irregular intervals and running from the facing into the centre of the core. When the wall had been built to the required height, a layer of fine concrete was laid down to form the rampart-walk and the outer face was finished off with a string-course made up from the usual tiles, or on occasion moulded tiles specially produced for the purpose. The structure which resulted was tough and durable, capable of withstanding the ravages of weather, the shock of earthquake and indeed almost everything but the depredations of modern man. The only blemish noticeable on most of the circuit is the tendency of the facing to draw away from the core, due to the lack of depth in many of the facing-tiles.

There is no certain indication of an earth rampart behind the wall at any point, and indeed the fact that the rear facing was treated in the same careful way as the front speaks clearly against the existence of such a feature. But in certain places, for example south of Porta Chiusa and in the Quartiere di San Saba, the wall stands immediately in front of a great mass of earth, as though it here fronted an earthwork.[15] There is, however, no good reason to suppose that these mounds are the remains of a man-made defence which has been removed or concealed elsewhere on the circuit. That is, in itself, inherently unlikely. More probably, these are natural features of the landscape against which the wall has been set to avoid too great a deviation from its planned course.

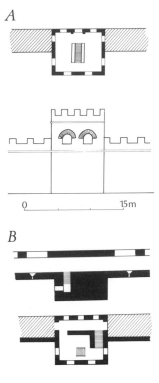

Fig. 12 Towers in Aurelian's wall between Porta Appia and Porta Ardeatina.

The towers

At regular intervals, the average interspace being about 30 m, towers were provided as part of the original building programme (fig. 12). In all, 381 seem to have existed along the greater part of the circuit, the only sector on which they were not thought to be necessary being that fronting the Tiber. The great majority of the Aurelianic towers were simply planned, in keeping with the economic policy adopted by Aurelian's building parties. The common type consisted of a solid mass of tile-faced concrete, 7·6 m long and projecting 3·35 m forward of the wall-face. This reached as high as the rampart-walk where it formed the base of a chamber which extended to the rear face of the wall. Each tower was roofed by a three-bayed barrel-vault, the central bay covering a staircase which gave access to the flat, battlemented top of the tower from the rampart-walk. The tower roof rose some 4·5 m higher than the top of the wall. The chamber was normally lit by two round-headed windows in the front wall, one at the back and one at each side (figs. 13 and 14).

The towers provided on the galleried wall were perforce differently planned, though their external aspect remained largely unaltered. These towers also projected 3·35 m in front of the wall and were solid to the level of the gallery-walk, i.e. to about 3 m. From the gallery, a staircase ran round three sides of the tower giving access to the chamber. This was of the same dimensions as in the majority of other towers but its internal arrangement was somewhat different, being cramped by the stair-well. In neither type of tower was there any means of access from the ground to the upper chamber. Access to the upper works could only be gained by stairs at the gates and the defenders

Fig. 13 Tower near Porta Appia, showing single blocked window. Usually there were two. (Photograph: Edwin Smith)

Fig. 14 Towers immediately south of Porta Tiburtina. (Fototeca Unione)

could pass along the wall only by the rampart-walk. The principal aim in this was presumably to keep unauthorized personnel from the walk and the towers where their presence might impede the defenders during an emergency.

There is little doubt that the Aurelianic towers were designed with the deployment of artillery, especially *ballistae*, in mind. The solid construction of the towers and the wide windows or casemates can best be explained in connexion with siege artillery. Space for two *ballistae* was available in most of the towers, although whether they were installed as permanent fixtures is very doubtful. It is most unlikely that a total of more than 700 machines, and the skilled crews to man and maintain them, would normally be available, either in Aurelian's day or later. (Of the place of artillery in late Roman fortification, see below p. 82.)

The gates

Of the eighteen gates envisaged in the original Aurelianic plan, nine have survived, though all have been substantially modified by later rebuilding. During the expansion of Rome between the sixteenth and nineteenth centuries, and the more rapid growth of the city since 1900, road-building and the accompanying piercing of the defences led to the loss of much which in detail can never be reconstructed. Fortunately, not all knowledge of the vanished gates is lost, for many of them were drawn by one or more artists who produced a splendid series of pictures of the gates. The process began in the earlier sixteenth century with Van Heemskerck, was continued by Dosio, Piranesi, Asselyn, Silvestre, Vasi and Cassini, to be superbly rounded off by the nineteenth-century engravings of Gell, Rossini and Ricciardelli. Early photographers, too, have played their part, notably J. H. Parker in his first and second folios of *Historical Photographs* (1870).[16] These records of what has perished suggest, so far as they are able, that the destroyed gates followed the same pattern of development as those which survive. As a result, the following discussion concentrates upon those which can still be seen.

The most notable feature of the Aurelianic gates as a class is their adherence to a standard. Clearly their builders were working to a carefully predetermined plan. The gates which lay on the major roads, Portae Appia, Flaminia, Ostiensis East and Portuensis, possessed double entrances, the other major gates only one, i.e. Portae Latina (fig. 16), Nomentana, Labicana and Salaria. Portae Tiburtina, Aurelia Pancraziana and Aurelia Sancti Petri probably also belonged to this group. Minor gates included Portae Metrobia, Ardeatina, Asinaria, Pinciana, Septimiana and Ostiensis West, these having single entrances and usually less elaborate towers and gate houses.

The gate towers in most cases appear to have possessed semicircular fronts in which were set a varying number of windows. Between the towers lay a two-storied curtain pierced by one or two entrances, according to the relative importance of the gate. The form of all the Aurelianic gates was fundamentally simple and, as will be seen later (p. 72), represents no break with a long tradition of gate architecture which reaches back to the beginnings of the Empire. Though the majority of the surviving gates follow the same pattern, there are a number of divergences from the norm, as was inevitable on such a long circuit. The most striking is the plan of Porta Asinaria (fig. 15). This was in origin a simple postern-gate set, not quite centrally, between two rectangular wall towers of which the southern example differed from the norm in having a staircase leading from the ground to the rampart-walk. The length of curtain between the towers is 30 m and the gate-opening only 4·5 m so that the passage was barely adequately covered. The towers cannot be seen as flanking the gate in any meaningful way and structurally they have nothing to do with it. The gate was clearly placed here to allow entry for the two roads

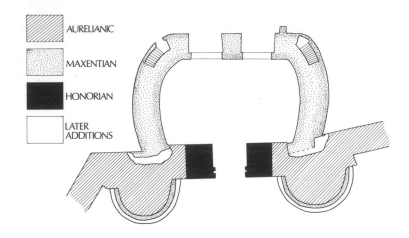

AURELIANIC

MAXENTIAN

HONORIAN

LATER
ADDITIONS

PORTA OSTIENSIS EAST

0 _____ 10 _____ 20 m

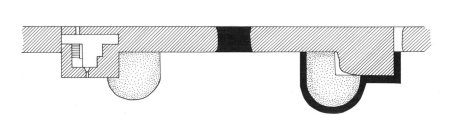

PORTA ASINARIA

Fig. 15 Plans of gates in Aurelian's wall, I: Porta Ostiensis East and Porta Asinaria.

Via Asinaria and Via Tusculana approaching the city from the south-east, but why a larger gate was not provided is not clear. This was presumably an economy measure, though why it was applied here and at no other point where a major road entered is unexplained. In a later rebuild, economy was abandoned and Porta Asinaria was brought into line with other major gates, while retaining its single entrance (below, p. 53).

Two other gates with features peculiar to themselves may be noted. At the Porta Pinciana (fig. 16) on the north side of the circuit the road approached the line of defences on an unusually oblique course. The line of the wall was accordingly offset at the gate to accommodate the road. The odd angle at

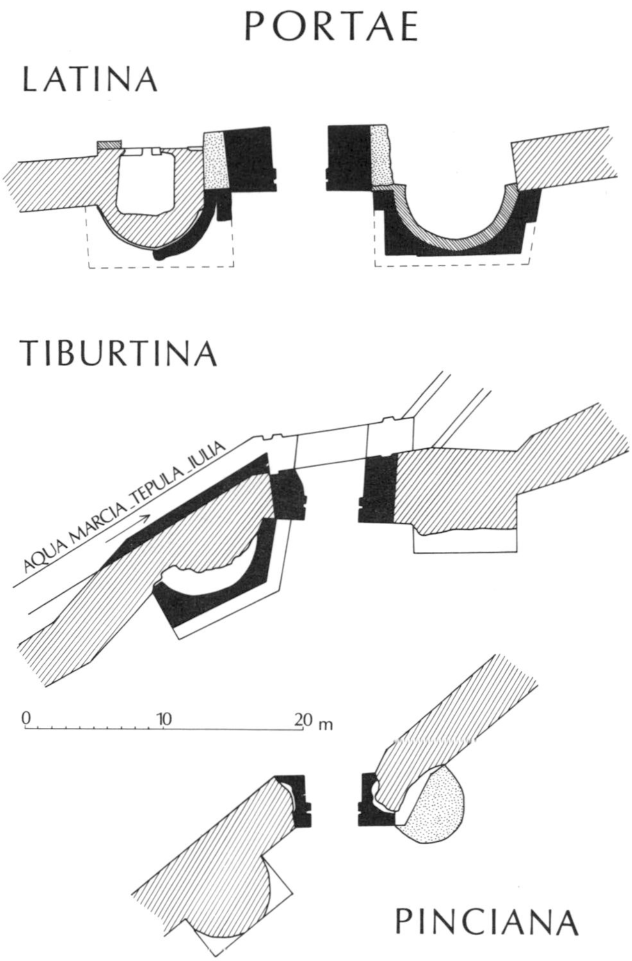

PORTAE

LATINA

TIBURTINA

AQUA MARCIA-TEPULA-IULIA

0 _____ 10 _____ 20 m

PINCIANA

Fig. 16 Plans of gates in Aurelian's wall, II: Porta Latina, Porta Tiburtina and Porta Pinciana. (For key, see fig. 15, p. 36)

which the roadway met the wall brought changes to the plan of the gate. The tower on the eastern side could not be built to the usual dimensions and is, in fact, only 7 m wide. The other tower was swept away in a later reconstruction but is unlikely to have been any larger. The form of the original gate house has also been lost due to later rebuilding, but like the structure which took its place it probably had a short curtain over a single narrow entrance and was probably set at right angles to the course of the road.

The fine gate which spanned the Via Tiburtina (figs. 16 and 18) on the east side of the city was placed immediately in front of an arch which, since the reign of Augustus, had carried the Aqua Marcia–Tepula–Iulia across the

Fig. 17 Exterior of Porta Latina. (Fototeca Unione)

same road. The Porta Tiburtina has been much altered since its original construction, both in the late Roman period and in the Middle Ages, but it is still clear that Aurelian's wall here changed its course to admit the road on a more convenient alignment. The Aurelianic gate towers have been almost entirely removed by later works but they seem to have had the customary semicircular fronts.

Among the gates which have now vanished, the Porta Praenestina–Labicana[17] (fig. 19) was also sited before a much earlier aqueduct arch, this time the great Claudian aqueduct known as Aqua Claudia and Aqua Anio Novus which carried its water-channel across the two roads Via Praenestina and Via Labicana (fig. 20). The gate also incorporated the late Republican tomb of Eurysaces the baker, and in 1838–9 Pope Gregory XVI ordered the late Imperial gate to be demolished so that the tomb and the splendid aqueduct arch might be made clearly visible. Though the surviving engravings of the gate do not reveal all the details of this complex structure, and are particularly inadequate on its original lay-out, it is apparent that in all periods this was an exceptional gateway. The two roads made for separate arches in the Claudian aqueduct, the tomb of Eurysaces lying between them. That massive structure, minus its front, was incorporated in a round-fronted tower, almost certainly dating from the time of Aurelian. The outstanding problem is by what means the two roadways were flanked. Square towers are shown in the appropriate positions in eighteenth- and early nineteenth-century drawings, but these are most probably structures of the fourth

Fig. 18 Exterior of Porta Tiburtina. (Fototeca Unione)

PORTA CHIUSA

PORTA NOMENTANA

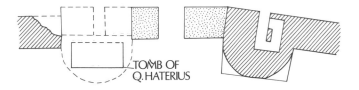

PORTA PRAENESTINA

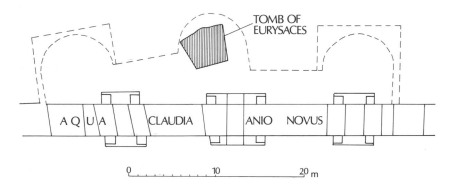

Fig. 19 Plans of gates in Aurelian's wall, III: Porta Chiusa, Porta Nomentana and Porta Praenestina. (For key, see fig. 15, p. 36)

Fig. 20 *opposite* Claudian aqueduct arch behind site of Porta Praenestina. In the background, the tomb of Eurysaces which may have been incorporated in the central tower of the gate. (Photograph: Edwin Smith)

century. Did they replace towers with the usual rounded fronts? This will never be known for certain but the gate structure thus completed would represent a logical and efficient solution to the problems set by the convergence of the two roads at the aqueduct. Nothing more can be learnt of the third-century gate but another feature of the Porta Praenestina–Labicana

Fig. 21 Blocked postern in the Licinian gardens, south of Porta Nomentana. (Fototeca Unione)

will be considered later, the surviving inscription of the emperor Honorius (below p. 65).

In addition to the gates a number of posterns were included in Aurelian's wall. The total originally existing is unknown but six can still be seen and a further five, all in the riverside wall, are listed in the Einsiedeln List, a ninth-century manuscript which records the major features of the wall for the benefit of pilgrims visiting Rome. All the existing posterns belong to a very simple type, their narrow openings being surmounted by flat lintels, and in two cases by flat arches, of travertine blocks. Above these door-heads were double relieving arches. All the posterns are now blocked and so their internal appearance is uncertain. Probably, however, their openings passed directly through the wall without offsets. All the posterns may have been blocked at the same time and this apparently occurred within a few decades of construction.

Certainly the postern at the Praetorian Camp can have had no function to fulfil after 312, when that fortress was largely dismantled. Apart from this postern, the surviving examples occur south of Porta Nomentana at the Licinian gardens (fig. 21) on the east side of the city, two at Vigna Casoli west of Porta Appia, and one at the Lateran Palace.

Also mentioned in the Einsiedeln List are the only other features of Aurelian's wall not yet described, the garderobes (*necessaria*). Very few of these still survive and it is far from clear how many of these, if any, belong to the original defences. Some twenty examples have been traced, chiefly through the remains of corbels supporting the projecting apses of the garderobes. Most if not all appear to belong to the later, galleried wall, but they probably took the place of earlier sanitary arrangements which have vanished without trace. It is possible, as Richmond suggested,[18] that the towers were originally equipped with one garderobe each, and there may have been similar provision at the gate towers. But at the gates, too, the precise form of the arrangements in the 270s is unknown.

Who was responsible for building the wall? No inscriptions whether military or civilian have come from the original work as a record of any part of the building operation, and Latin literary sources are silent on the question. The Byzantine writer John Malalas,[19] active in the later sixth century, does however report that Aurelian himself presided over the operation and compelled the city *collegia* (or guild-corporations) to carry out the work. The historical value of this statement has been doubted by some, but it contains nothing unlikely or unreasonable. Clearly the number of soldiers available to Aurelian will have been negligible, though presumably specialist military engineers were consulted at the stage of planning. Of civil organizations within the city, the *collegia* alone would seem to offer an appropriately large labour-force and one, moreover, already accustomed to providing compulsory labour for official purposes. Malalas' report seems unlikely to be mere invention and may be given credence in the absence of any more specific testimony.

The riverside wall and the defences around Trastevere

Aurelian's builders included within their fortification a salient west of the Tiber (the district now known as Trastevere, and the Augustan Fourteenth Region of the city), a densely peopled area which includes several important structures. The evidence for assigning the encircling of this region to Aurelian's reign once again lies in finds recovered from buildings which had to make way for the defences. In 1878–80, excavations of an Imperial wine warehouse (the *Cellae Vinariae Novae et Arruntianae*) in the grounds of the

Villa Farnesina at the northern end of this salient revealed that this second-century building had lost its double portico to the wall and to private houses later erected within its shelter. Coins from these domestic buildings extended down to the early fourth century; but, within the west bank area surrounded by the wall, occupation continued during the fifth and sixth centuries.[20]

Three gates existed in the wall around Trastevere, Portae Portuensis, Aurelia–Pancraziana and Septimiana, all of them now vanished from sight. Of Porta Septimiana virtually nothing is known apart from its site, the gate having been thoroughly reconstructed in the late fifteenth century. Even its name provokes a problem, a connection with the Emperor Septimius Severus seeming colourable only if an earlier arch of his time had been incorporated in the wall.[21] Knowledge of the other two gates is more satisfactory, for they survived until new fortifications were built in the 1640s by Pope Urban VIII. Drawings of the sixteenth and seventeenth centuries demonstrate that Porta Portuensis possessed a double-arched opening flanked by semicircular towers, like the other Aurelianic gates on major roads, and also that it was distinguished by the addition of an imposing honorific inscription in the early fifth century (below p. 65). Porta Aurelia–Pancraziana was a less important, and thus smaller, opening, a single arch set between rectangular brick towers apparently of the same type as those on the wall circuit.

The wall which ran along the east bank of the Tiber is very poorly represented by finds and records. Even its precise course cannot be traced with certainty. Archaeological evidence for its date is thus sparse and the principal testimony for its place in the structural history of the defences of Rome is that of the sixth-century writer Procopius, who plainly regarded it as of the same date as the wall around Trastevere, that is of the later third century,[22] and this must be accepted as most probable from the point of view of tactics. A river frontage devoid of protection would have been unthinkable. It is not clear beyond doubt whether or not towers existed on the river wall. A passage of Procopius might be taken to indicate that they were absent.

Since the Romans of former times, trusting to the Tiber channel, had built the wall without care, constructing it low and without towers, Witigis [the leader of the besieging Goths] hoped to take the city easily from this side.[23]

But the Einsiedeln List gives sixteen towers in the riverside sector and this is not a source to be lightly rejected. Possibly, then, the towers were more widely spaced here than elsewhere, or one stretch of river wall was left entirely without towers. The matter must be left there for the present, pending systematic excavation or a fortunate discovery.

The final feature of note in the riverside defences is a strongpoint built around the Mausoleum of Hadrian. Only one major bridge lay beyond the protection of the wall, the Pons Aelius. Immediately across the bridge on the west bank lay the great brick drum of Hadrian's Mausoleum (the Castel St Angelo of medieval Rome). By the sixth century, as Procopius describes, this structure had become a bridgehead fort surrounded by strong walls, and as such attracted the attention of the besieging Goths. Unfortunately, Procopius did not know, or at least does not say, when the Mausoleum was first turned over to its new function and no archaeological light has been thrown on the matter. In the absence of real evidence one can do no more than state possibilities. On the one hand, there is the strong presumptive argument that the Pons Aelius was guarded in some definite way in the later third century. On the other, there is no proof that a fortification was erected here so early: all that Procopius says is that 'the Romans of old' had made the tomb part of their city wall. There are several possible occasions for the conversion to a bridgehead fort, from the later third to the fifth centuries, among which the claims of Aurelian's reign remain far from insignificant.[24]

3

The walls from Maxentius to Belisarius

The reorganization of Maxentius

The threat of barbarian invasion which prompted the building of Aurelian's great wall around Rome did not materialize. By the time the wall was completed the most serious years of crisis were past and several decades of recovery and reorganization were to ensue under the direction, first, of Diocletian and his colleagues in two Tetrarchies, later of Constantine the Great. The wall of Aurelian was not long to remain in its original state, but when major changes were made to it they were occasioned not by external foes but by the conflicting ambitions of rival Roman rulers. Not for the first time, nor the last, physical possession of *Urbs Roma* was the required object of a claimant for power, its acquisition setting the final seal upon his right to rule the Roman world. In order to appreciate the historical background to the first modifications to Aurelian's defences, it is necessary to sketch in briefly the outline of the New Order which Diocletian's reforms brought into being.

Shortly after his accession in 283, Diocletian chose as his co-partner in Empire Maximian, giving him special responsibility for the western provinces. From 293 these two senior emperors, or Augusti, were assisted by two subordinates, Caesars, Constantius Chlorus in the west, Galerius in the east, the two Caesars being designated to succeed the Augusti in due course. While Diocletian's dominating personality was everywhere felt, the system (if it may be so described) held together. But in 305 he abdicated and caused Maximian to do the same.

In the following year Constantius, now the western Augustus, died and the army in Britain hailed his son Constantine as his successor. In Rome, meanwhile, Maximian was recalled to power by his son Maxentius, who defeated and killed the duly appointed western Caesar, Severus, in 307 when the latter threatened to march on the city. Other usurpations and appointments meant that at one time there were no less than seven Augusti ruling in different parts of the Empire, instead of the intended two. Rome itself was held from 306 to 312 by Maxentius, who not only beat off Severus in 307 but later in the same year prevented the eastern Augustus, Galerius, from taking the city. On both these occasions Maxentius appears to have based his successful strategy upon the impregnability of the Aurelianic defences, keeping the bulk of his forces well within the circuit. A third assault on Rome came in 312, led this time by Constantine and his western armies, and for some inexplicable reason Maxentius did not, as earlier, trust to the walls. Instead he allowed a substantial part of his forces to be drawn into battle at the Milvian bridge, presumably believing that his numerically superior army would sweep aside the invaders. But the altered strategy failed. Constantine's troops carried the day and took Rome.

The literary sources for the years 306–12 have nothing specific to say about the part played in these events by the Aurelianic defences or about any changes made to them by Maxentius. The only statement bearing on these years tells us that Maxentius 'began the digging of a ditch but did not complete it' (Lactantius, *de morte persecutorum* 27). By itself this statement could not be taken to indicate building activity on the wall: ditch-digging alone is specified, not mural fortification. But there is evidence from the wall itself of a major scheme of rebuilding, involving the curtains, towers and gates, and a variety of considerations points to the near-certain conclusion that it was carried out in the early fourth century, i.e. in the reign of Maxentius. First, the scheme of work certainly dates from *before* the reign of Honorius (A.D. 393–423). In that reign a distinctive programme of work was carried out on the gates in particular, as a group of inscriptions clearly demonstrates (below p. 64), and it is beyond question that the Honorian work postdates the changes now being considered. This is an important fixed point in the history of Rome's defences, for in only one period before Honorius was the city seriously threatened, and that was in the reign of Maxentius. Secondly, from three places in the fabric of this second phase of construction there have been recovered stamped tiles dating from the first decade of the fourth century.[25] One of the findspots lay in the heightening of the curtain wall east of Porta Ostiensis East, another from the blocking of Porta Ostiensis West. Both sets of tiles are thus associated with major measures of defence which may reasonably be linked with the provision of a ditch as mentioned by Lactantius. The third findspot, outside the north-east angle of *Castra Praetoria*, adds nothing to the argument one way or another. Thirdly, the character of the brickwork accords closely with structures known to date from the early fourth century, most notably with the great Basilica of Maxentius. Finally, as Richmond[26] convincingly argued, the new form of the city defences finds an appropriate context in the assertive building programme carried through in a surprisingly short space of time by Maxentius, thereby justifying his claim to be *Conservator Urbis Suae*.

We may now turn back to the wall and examine the Maxentian changes in detail, beginning with the curtain-wall itself.

The wall
It has already been pointed out (above p. 28) that the wall shows two main

Fig. 22 Interior of galleried wall, between Porta Latina and Porta Ardeatina. (Fototeca Unione)

Fig. 23 Rear of galleried wall from the Protestant Cemetery. (Courtauld Institute)

phases of construction, the earlier, solid wall of Aurelian's original scheme, the later, a galleried structure, usually some 8 m high, with a broad wall to the front and a continuous arcade on the inner side (figs. 10C, 22 and 23). This galleried wall, as has been argued, is assignable to the Maxentian occupation of Rome between 306 and 312. Over the gallery ran a rampart-walk, a little more than 3 m wide, fronted by a parapet and merlons. In the front face of the gallery, narrow slit-windows occurred at irregular intervals. The total height of the wall from footings to merlons was now more than 15 m, and in some places nearly 20 m. The constructional details of the new work were broadly similar to those of the original structure, though the facing-tiles were not so scrupulously chosen, the joints between tiles and junctions between units were less regular, and bonding courses were omitted. This minor decline from the high standards evident in Aurelian's wall is probably to be attributed to haste rather than to mere negligence or bad workmanship, but in any case these deficiencies should not be overemphasized. The overall standard of the work is still consistently high for so massive an undertaking.

As in the wall of the first period, the Maxentian work was not entirely uniform in construction throughout its entire length. Although its character along most of the circuit was as has been outlined above, in a few sectors it took a different form. In those stretches where the Aurelianic wall was backed by a mass of earth (above p. 31), the new upper wall measured no more than 2 m in thickness and was positioned on the front of the earlier work, thus leaving some 2 m to the rear as a rampart-walk. No gallery was included in these sectors. In one stretch where no rearward earth bank existed, immediately in front of the aqueducts Marcia, Tepula and Iulia on the eastern side of the city, the same type of upper wall was built, for reasons which are now obscure. Another variant form existed in the south-west corner of the circuit, where the wall ran in front of the two aqueducts Anio Novus and Claudia. The Maxentian wall reached to the level of the Aqua Claudia; to support the new structure the first period wall was extended to the rear, and buttresses were placed on the extension against the rear of the heightened wall. The towers in this sector had been sited between the piers of the aqueducts so that access to the later wall could be had from these without the users climbing over or walking on the aqueduct channels. This unusually elaborate arrangement was thus a painstaking device to ensure that the flow of water in these two conduits was in no way interfered with.

Now that the defences had been raised to a height of more than 15 m, the city possessed a protective shield which only the most determined and prolonged siege could hope to pierce. The galleried wall meant that men, materials and machines could be rushed to whatever sector required them, with far greater despatch than a besieging force could hope to match. Further, the enormous height of the upper rampart-walk gave not only improved range and vision to the defenders: it also enabled a smaller number of them to engage and hold down an attacking group, thus allowing greater flexibility of movement among those manning the wall. It is difficult to see how any ancient army could invest and take by siege operations an *enceinte* of this scale on an 18 km circuit. The later history of Rome was to prove the truth of this and the worth of the wall of Aurelian and Maxentius.

The towers
Inevitably the heightening of the wall brought changes to the towers, since the curtain now rose to the level of the tower roofs. But in the case of many of the towers, the resultant modifications were inconsiderable. In a number of surviving examples it is clear that the Maxentian builders left the Aurelianic towers much as they were, so that their flat roofs projected forward of the wall at the same level as the parapet. Others, however, were substantially enlarged to take account of the new curtain at the rear. In many, a large chamber covered by a hipped roof was built over the older flat roof, the parapet and

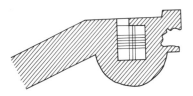
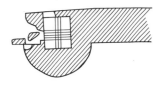

AURELIANIC

0   10   20 m

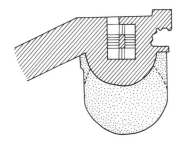
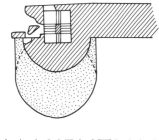

MAXENTIAN

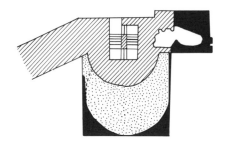
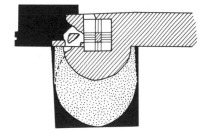

HONORIAN

PORTA APPIA

Fig. 24 Structural development of the Porta Appia.

merlons having been removed and the windows below them blocked. The new upper chamber contained normally three round-headed windows in front, one to each side and two at the back, with a door giving access to the curtain-wall. In a smaller number of cases a more radical rebuilding was carried out. The old upper works were taken down to the level of the former flat roof. Over this was then erected a new storey, covered like the other heightened towers with a hipped roof.

The different treatment given to the towers by the Maxentian builders is remarkable. A large number were not significantly altered at all and relatively few were substantially enlarged. There are no discernible tactical or topographical reasons for this inconsistency and in seeking the underlying cause we should probably associate the variable treatment accorded to the towers with what seem to be signs of haste in the construction of the upper curtain-wall. It would not be surprising if this ambitious scheme, begun not before 306 (and most probably in 307 when the first threat came to Rome), was still incomplete in 312 when Constantine's army arrived from the north. If the building of the new wall and the towers (and the gates) had been continuing *pari passu*, it would well explain why, when the third and final threat to Maxentius' rule came, so many of the towers had perforce to be left at their original height. Six years was all too short a space of time for what Maxentius had in mind. A decade at least would have been a more reasonable span.

The gates

The second phase of construction at the gates is also to be ascribed to the reign of Maxentius. Two gates in particular, Porta Appia and Porta Asinaria, received special treatment and were now transformed into towering and magnificent structures, marking a significant departure from the dignified but strictly utilitarian gates of Aurelian. Two other gates, Porta Latina and Porta Ostiensis East, were modified on their inner sides but externally were hardly altered at all. The great majority of the other gates, where surviving remains allow their building history to be studied, were little changed from their Aurelianic form, except where change was necessary to conform to the new higher wall. The intention of the Maxentian builders can best be judged by examination of the Porta Appia and Porta Asinaria, and it is here that we will begin.

In its early fourth-century form, Porta Appia was to become the most splendid of the gates of Rome (figs. 24, 25 and 26). Its massive remains form the most complicated of Roman monuments and the disentangling of their building sequence is one of Richmond's finest achievements in observation and record. The Maxentian workmen utterly transformed the Aurelianic gate by adding to the earlier work lofty, four-storied towers with rounded fronts,

Fig. 25 Exterior of the Porta Appia. (Fototeca Unione)

24 m in height and 13 m deep. The new galleried wall now adjoined the gate towers at the level of their third storey, that is at the height of the late third-century gate curtain which was still retained in use. A courtyard was constructed to the rear of the gate and from it staircases led up to the new towers. At the back of this court lay an archway associated with an older aqueduct, the Aqua Antoniniana, and this was made to do duty as the somewhat elegant entrance to the new courtyard.

The Porta Asinaria (figs. 27, 28, 29 and 30), the most unusual of the Aurelianic gates, consisting of a plain single entrance set in the space between two of the wall towers, was also drastically altered. Round-fronted towers were added to those sides of the earlier rectangular towers nearest to the gate-opening, the new towers (and the old) being raised in four stories to a height of

Fig. 26 Rear of the Porta Appia around 1870, showing arch of Aqua Antoniniana. (Fototeca Unione)

Fig. 27 *opposite* Porta Asinaria, showing rectangular Aurelianic towers and Maxentian round-fronted additions. (Mansell Collection)

18·5 m. The curtain between the towers rose almost to the level of their topmost storey and twin guard-posts were sited on the sentry-walk. These are unusual features in late Roman fortification and elsewhere on the Roman circuit are found only at Porta Ostiensis East.

None of the other gates was distinguished in this monumental fashion by the Maxentian builders. That Porta Appia should have been marked out for a magnificent rebuilding is not surprising, since it spanned one of the major roads leading to the south. But the Via Asinaria possessed no such

Fig. 28 Exterior of Porta Asinaria, showing Maxentian towers and Honorian stone curtain. (Fototeca Unione)

importance. Why then was its gate raised to such dignity? The most probable explanation is that the Maxentian scheme intended most of the city gates to be enlarged in this manner. Urgent military consideration led the builders to concentrate their energies on the wall and, to a lesser extent, on the towers, so that work on only two gates had advanced by the time that Constantine's victory in 312 brought Maxentius' programme to a halt. This still does not adequately explain why the Asinarian Gate was chosen for rebuilding early in the series, rather than for example Porta Latina or Porta Tiburtina. On so long a circuit it is probable that the ready availability of personnel and building materials played an important role in the phasing of the work programme. If, as seems likely, work gangs were assigned to particular sectors, it may well be that progress on the wall in the two southern sectors which included these two gates had advanced so far that here alone could work begin on gate construction. But other interpretations are possible, including Richmond's suggestion[27] that these two gates were chosen because they lay on roads leading to the new Circus of Maxentius from populous parts of the city.

Work of this second period at the other gates was relatively minor in scope and significance, though all were presumably modified to suit the heightened wall. Perhaps the most radical change took place at Porta Ostiensis East, where the tower fronts were refaced and the upper stories rebuilt and a large inner court added (figs. 31 and 32). This had its own imposing rear entrance with two passageways. A somewhat less impressive inner court was also built

Fig. 29 Rear of Porta Asinaria. (Fototeca Unione)

Fig. 30 Porta Asinaria: east gate tower in the Maxentian gate. (Photograph: D. J. Watts)

behind Porta Latina but this gate was otherwise little affected. Elsewhere, the Maxentian alterations were of a similarly minor order, except perhaps at the small Porta Pinciana (fig. 16), where a round-fronted tower was built on the west side of the gate at the same time as the wall was heightened. It is possible that these finishing-off tasks were performed after 312 by Constantine rather than by the Maxentian workmen but the point is not certain.

This concludes the analysis of the second period changes to the defences. The evidence from the wall, its towers and its gates indicates a falling-off in the execution of a grand design formulated by Maxentius as one element in a splendid building programme which also included the great Basilica, a Circus by the Appian Way and the restoration of the temple of Venus and Rome. The repair of Italian roads was also actively pursued during his short regime. In about 310, only four years after the work on the wall started, it must have been clear that time would not allow its completion before Constantine made an attempt to seize Rome, as he did two years later. By then, the new wall had taken shape but work on the towers and gates was nowhere near the final stages. Even the digging of the surrounding ditch was not complete. It follows that some building operations remained to be carried out after 312 by Constantine. The ditch, at least, would presumably have been finished, and work may have continued at some of the gates, though there is no sign that Constantine intended to implement in full the Maxentian plans for the gates and towers.

The restoration by Honorius in the early fifth century

After the Maxentian transformation of the defences of Rome there appears to have been no work of building or reconstruction for some ninety years. For the rest of the fourth century, Rome was not seriously threatened either by barbarian intruders or by some claimant to Imperial power. The next occasion for modifications to the wall was in the context of an incursion of Goths at the beginning of the fifth century, the first time that invaders from the north had ranged widely in the Italian peninsula since Hannibal's army in the late third century B.C.

In A.D. 400 a large Gothic army was led into Italy by Alaric. They passed around the Julian Alps and entered the valley of the Izono, threatening the great city and port of Aquileia and a little later Ravenna. Aquileia may have fallen to Alaric, who then turned westwards towards Milan where the emperor Honorius and his court were in residence at this time. Milan did not fall to the Goths, but the mere presence of a large invading force on the soil of Italy, and immediately outside the gates of some of her great cities, spread alarm throughout the peninsula and even a city as powerfully defended as Rome was not felt by its citizenry to be impregnable. The defence of Italy lay in the hands

of the capable Vandal commander Stilicho whose determined resistance in two engagements, at Pollentia and at Verona in the spring of 403, convinced Alaric that further successes in Italy would not for the moment be forthcoming. He withdrew beyond the Alps to await a later opportunity.

The alarm felt in Rome as Alaric's army swept from Aquileia across to Milan and on to Pollentia led those responsible for the city's defence to make still more formidable the already immensely strong walls. But even in what seemed at the time desperate circumstances, attention was paid to the appearance of the defences, especially the gates, as well as to their purely defensive capability. These changes were to be the last major work of an emperor on the walls of Rome and it is entirely fitting that they should have added dignity as well as strength to the defences.

The restoration carried out in the reign of Honorius is mentioned by the contemporary court-poet, Claudian, whose panegyric verses are a primary, though infuriatingly vague, source for the momentous first years of the fifth century. More important for the matter of chronology, three inscriptions can be linked with work on the wall occasioned by the Gothic threat, the first, and indeed the only, epigraphic records directly associated with the defences of Imperial Rome.[28] Claudian's lines (de VI Consulatu Honorii 529–34) indicate that the building work began at the end of 401 when the first intelligence of the Gothic invasion reached Rome. With this dating the main texts of the three surviving inscriptions agree closely, since one of them mentions the eastern emperor Theodosius II who was raised to that position in February 402 following the death of Arcadius. At the latest then the dedicatory inscriptions must have been cut before early March 402. The emergency was to last for sixteen months in all, until Stilicho's victory at Pollentia on Easter Day 403 brought proof that Alaric could be stopped. After Pollentia, work seems to have ceased, even though certain tasks were still incomplete.

Little new work was carried out on the wall, the programme being essentially one of repair and restoration. The basic structure of the wall appears, in any case, to have needed relatively little attention considering that it was now 130 years old. The towers, too, were not greatly altered, beyond the replacement of the windows by narrow loop-holes wherever this could be conveniently effected. Once again it is the gates in which the new mode makes its most striking impact. All the double-portalled gates on the main roads, with the single exception of Porta Portuensis, were apparently now reduced to

Fig. 31 *opposite top* Exterior of Porta Ostiensis East. (Fototeca Unione)

Fig. 32 *opposite bottom* Rear of Porta Ostiensis East, showing Maxentian rebuilding of the upper stories and the addition of an inner courtyard. (Fototeca Unione)

Fig. 33 Porta Appia: portcullis slot in the early fifth-century gate. (Photograph: D. J. Watts)

a single entrance. These were Portae Appia, Flaminia, and Ostiensis East (see above p. 35). This reduction was effected by the insertion of single-arched gateways of stone, one storey in height, each provided with a portcullis (fig. 33). The stone appears to have been derived from earlier buildings, now demolished. These entrances to Rome now measured only about 4 m in width. The Honorian single portals in stone can be best seen today in Porta Appia and Porta Ostiensis East (figs. 25 and 31). The earlier narrow gates were also included in the work of blocking. Porta Tiburtina had its portal reduced to a

Fig. 34 Interior of Porta Chiusa, showing Maxentian blocking. (After F. Cicconetti, 1869)

similar width of 4 m, while Porta Asinaria was blocked altogether by brickwork, never to be reopened. The little Porta Chiusa (figs. 19 and 34), which had been narrowed by Maxentius to only 3·6 m, was now also entirely blocked and never again used. All the surviving single-arch gates and several of those which have now vanished were provided with curtains in travertine marble and it is reasonably certain that all the gates were given this sober embellishment.

But the most profound and enduring alteration was wrought in the towers of many of the gates. The semicircular-fronted towers of Aurelian's gates were in many cases incorporated within new towers of rectangular plan and built of stone. Essentially, all that this meant was that the semicircular towers were given a solid facing of re-used stone, but the combined effect of the new-style towers and the stone curtains was not only to strengthen but to enhance the external appearance of these gates and carry them to a new level of architectural expression. For there can be little doubt that the intention was to make the city gates as handsome as possible and not merely powerful. Nowhere is this more clearly seen than at Porta Appia (fig. 25) (and, before its demolition, at Porta Flaminia), where the entrance was flanked by towers clad in white marble. It is extraordinary that, given the circumstances of their building, so much time and attention should have been lavished on these stones and marble facings. But so it was, and these Honorian gateways may justly be regarded as the last representatives in Imperial Rome of that ancient tradition of triumphal entrances to a city. Fittingly, Honorius must have entered the *Urbs* through one of them when he paid his triumphal first visit to Rome in 404, after the frustration of the first Gothic invasion of Italy.

A small number of gates were exempted from the main programme or were accorded somewhat different treatment. Porta Salaria and Porta Nomentana were not given new facings in stone, though the former gate was heightened by an extra storey, as was Porta Pinciana. At Porta Ostiensis East the new-style facing was applied but to the old semicircular-fronted towers: an extra storey was also added here. There was, then, no concerted attempt at uniformity and even if there had been it would have been frustrated by the fact that the scheme of work was left in an unfinished state. Porta Appia was not quite completed: the towers of Porta Latina were only partly built: the north tower of Porta Tiburtina was unfinished. All the same, much had been achieved in less than a year and a half, and these works must have severely taxed a distracted and hard-pressed population.

The ceremonial character of the Honorian treatment of the gates was further emphasized, in certain cases at least, by the handsome inscriptions on their stone curtains (see above p. 47). Three instances are known, of which one, on Porta Tiburtina, remains *in situ*, and another, from Porta Praenestina, survives in part and has been reconstructed at the site of the gate. The third, at Porta Portuensis, was destroyed along with the gate itself in 1643. All three texts agree closely with each other, reading as follows.

S   P   Q   R

IMPP CAESS DD NN INVICTISSIMIS PRINCIPIBVS ARCADIO ET
HONORIO VICTORIBVS AC TRIVMFATORIBVS SEMPER AVGG

OB INSTAVRATOS VRBI AETERNAE MVROS PORTAS AC TVRRES EGESTIS
INMENSIS RVDERIBVS EX SVGGESTIONE VC ET INLVSTRIS

COMITIS ET MAGISTRI VTRIVSQ MILITIAE STILICHONIS AD
PERPETVITATEM NOMINIS EORVM SIMVLACRA CONSTITVIT

CVRANTE FL MACROBIO LONGINIANO VC PRAEF VRBIS
D   N   M   Q   EORVM

The Senate and People of Rome to the Imperial Caesars, Our Lords, Unconquered Leaders, Arcadius and Honorius, Victorious and Triumphant, Eternal Emperors, for restoring the Walls, Gates and Towers of the Eternal City, after removing masses of stone débris, at the behest of Stilicho, Most Distinguished, Illustrious Count and Master of Two Commands, to the perpetuation of their Name, set up statues. Under the charge of Flavius Macrobius Longinianus, Most Distinguished, Prefect of the City, dedicated to their Divine Majesties.

In two of the texts (from Portae Tiburtina and Portuensis), the names of Stilicho and Macrobius Longinianus were erased after the fall of Stilicho in 408. The sense of the texts is clear enough but for the phrase *egestis immensis ruderibus*, 'after removing masses of stone débris'. It is not easy to see what this may mean. It has been taken to indicate the removal of rubbish which had accumulated against the wall close to the gates, but this is not certain. It is also puzzling that such a workaday phrase, describing such a menial task, should be commemorated in so honorific an inscription. It remains without convincing explanation. The statues of Arcadius and Honorius mentioned by the inscriptions have entirely vanished and nothing is known of them. They probably graced the stone curtains rather than the towers.

From Honorius to Belisarius

The defences of Rome received their first serious trial during Alaric's second invasion of Italy in 408–10. The Gothic leader again led his army into the peninsula in the autumn of 408, this time by-passing the northern cities and heading directly for Rome. Nothing stood in his way and in due course the city was under blockade. But the defences held firm: indeed there is no evidence that Alaric attempted to storm them. As early winter drew on, hunger and disease began to demoralize the city population and by December their leaders were ready to buy Alaric off with a vast hoard of treasure and luxury goods, silks, skins and pepper. The Goths withdrew northwards but to no great distance. A year later they again besieged Rome in order to enforce the treaty arrangements agreed in 408 and to avenge what Alaric claimed were insults to his dignity. Again the Romans were to suffer from starvation but Alaric's attention was distracted from the city by other objectives and again he withdrew his forces.

The emperor Honorius had spent much of the past few years, including the period when Rome was most seriously threatened, safe behind the walls and surrounding marshes of Ravenna. In the summer of 410 he and Alaric had a conference close to the city in an attempt to settle their differences. The negotiations were interrupted and Alaric again marched south and invested Rome for the third time. The siege was not long protracted. On 24 August, the Goths broke in at Porta Salaria under cover of darkness and for the next two or three days the city was given over to pillage before Alaric once more withdrew, this time heading south probably with the intention of seizing the all-important African grain supplies. The damage caused by this capture of Rome was no doubt great but three days was scarcely enough time for the Goths to destroy extensive areas of buildings. There is certainly no indication of damage to the defences at this time and it is most unlikely that the demolition of part of the massive works would have appealed to warriors who had only achieved their goal after two years of hard travail.

For the first time since their inception, the walls had fallen to assault. But there must linger a suspicion, already abroad in the sixth century if not earlier, that the Gothic entry was assisted from within. This cannot be proved, but is by no means unlikely. The citizenry of Rome had suffered much from privation and none can have relished the idea of a third blockade. The break-in at Porta Salaria on 24 August 410 need not imply that the defensive scheme had in any way failed. In the confused conditions of the day, hunger and demoralization are at least as likely to have let in the Goths as any flaw in the city defences.

Subsequent alterations to the walls were to be matters of repair and refurbishing rather than substantive reconstruction. After a major earthquake in 442, which damaged many buildings including the Colosseum, large cracks appeared in the southern sector of the wall between Porta Appia and Porta Metrobia. Porta Appia itself, whose massive towers had showed alarming cracks even before this time, was affected by the earthquake and required major repairs. These were carried out in courses of travertine blocks laid between bands of tile-facing. Despite the evidence of instability in this gate, an extra storey was added to the towers, probably immediately after 442. Certain parts of the wall and towers were now given buttresses, notably to the east of Porta Latina and of Porta Appia.

The final repairs, which can be linked with known historical events, are those associated with the Byzantine commander Belisarius in the period 536–46. Against the threat of Gothic armies he reconstructed those parts of the walls which had suffered damage or decay, providing for them a merlon with a short wall at the side to cover the exposed left side of the defender, a defensive device not hitherto used on the walls of Rome. He also dug a ditch or ditches around the city, of which no trace now survives. In front of the gates, or some of them, large man-traps were dug. All this is told us by the sixth-century writer Procopius[29] who fortunately had a great interest in military affairs. Procopius also tells us that large *ballistae* equipped with steel springs were installed in the tower and that small stone-throwing *onagri* were used on the wall. Both machines were an important factor in the successful defence against the besiegers. The powerful new *ballistae* played havoc with the Gothic machinery, which was in any case held at some distance from the wall by the new ditch-system. After the Goths withdrew, further repairs took place before the city was again in peril. At the end of 546, a Gothic force under Totila was by treachery allowed to break into the city at Porta Asinaria. Totila, recognizing the immense strength of the wall, set about demolishing it, but did not proceed far with the work before Belisarius recovered Rome in 547. The damage caused by Totila's men, and damage in other sectors, was restored, and some of these repairs can still be seen in the facing of the wall, where re-used blocks of stone and marble have been thrust into the gashed fabric. At the towers, a botching job was carried out, the stone blocks being simply pushed up against the earlier facing to form a kind of buttress. Most of these sixth-century accretions have now been removed.

Summary of the building sequence

A.D. 271 Aurelian began the construction of the defences, the work being carried out by the city *collegia*. The *enceinte* was to include 18 gates, 5 posterns and 381 towers. The work was completed in the reign of Aurelian's successor Probus.

306–12 Maxentius raised the wall in height by adding a galleried structure to the Aurelianic work. The wall now measured up to 20 m high, thus making necessary an increase in the height of the towers. Porta Appia and Porta Asinaria were also greatly heightened at this date. The digging of a ditch was begun but not completed.

401–4 Honorius instituted repairs and restoration to the wall, towers and gates. All the gates with double entrances were now reduced to a single portal by the insertion of well-constructed travertine gate houses. Porta Asinaria was entirely blocked up, as was the small Porta Chiusa. The towers of most of the gates were encased in stone, all of it apparently re-used. The major gates, at least, were embellished with statuary and honorific inscriptions.

410   The defences were pierced for the first time, by Alaric.

442   Damage by earthquake necessitated repairs to the south sector. An extra storey was added to Porta Appia and buttresses to certain stretches of the wall.

536–46 Belisarius repaired damaged sectors and added a ditch or ditches outside. Large *ballistae* were installed in the towers.

546   Totila broke in at Porta Asinaria and later attempted to demolish parts of the wall.

547   Belisarius recovered Rome and restored the fortifications.

4
Aurelian's wall in the development of Roman fortification

We may now turn to the development of fortifications from the early Empire[30] to that period of change, in castrametation and the defence of cities, in the middle of which Aurelian's wall was built. The modes of fortification current in the early Empire were created and disseminated by two main agencies: the Roman army, building for its garrisons temporary camps and permanent forts and fortresses in frontier areas, and Roman cities, especially colonial foundations, not infrequently established in territory only recently acquired and thus requiring some protective shield. Though these defences, and particularly those of cities, appear to have owed much to the influence of Hellenistic military engineers, relatively few well-dated instances of Roman fortifications from before the later first century B.C. have been studied, so that their derivation from earlier traditions cannot yet be clearly and convincingly traced.

The two agencies referred to must not be conceived of as following distinct and parallel paths. For in actuality military engineers *(architectus)* were employed in planning the defensive circuits of forts and cities alike, and other skilled military craftsmen were widely used in both spheres. Thus the strictly functional aspects of defences are strikingly to the fore in the early Empire. Nevertheless, among the builders of walls in many early Imperial cities, there were those who would have agreed with Aristotle that a wall should be an ornament as well as a protection (*Politics* vii, 10, 8).

The basic elements in the defensive arrangements provided for late Republican and Augustan colonies were a stone wall, normally but not invariably backed by an earth rampart, and one or more ditches outside it. Towers might be provided along the walls and at the angles but many cities managed without them. When present, they did not project massively in front of the wall curtain. Gates were usually simple, their single or double passages being flanked by towers linked by a parapet-walk over the gate-opening. The outline of the circuit of walls was rarely regular: oval, polygonal and still more irregular circuits were quite frequent. Now and again, as at Aosta (Augusta Praetoria) and Turin (Augusta Taurinorum) in northern Italy, the studious regularity of the walled area, and of the street-grid within, call to mind the lay-out of a military encampment and serve as a reminder that when these cities were founded in the early reign of Augustus, the territory in which they lay was not yet bound to Rome by a long tradition of loyalty. Elaboration in planning and in architectural detail was rare, although in some of the Italian cities the gates were made as imposing as possible. Excellent examples are the Porta Palatina at Turin, the Porta Praetoria at Aosta and the Porta Venere at Spello (Hispellum).

At this early date the defences of cities demanded much more of the engineers and their work gangs than the contemporary military works. The armies in the frontier provinces were building forts and fortresses with defences in turf and timber, and incorporating gates and internal buildings of timber also. Not until the reign of Claudius (A.D. 41–54) do we begin to find instances of stone fortifications but, even when introduced, they did not immediately spread to every frontier. In Germany timber forts were still common in the period A.D. 70–100. In Britain stone fortifications were provided for the legionary fortresses early in the second century and gradually for auxiliary forts thereafter. Along the Danube, too, there was a gradual introduction of stone defences from the mid first century, but examples in turf-work and timber are still found in the second century.

Though there is a multiplicity of variants in features such as gates and towers, military fortifications of the early Empire display a degree of uniformity which can still astound. From the Sahara fringe to Scotland, from Syria to Spain, the same types of fortification can be traced, modified but never masked by local differences in materials and constructional details. These were fortifications erected in a time of confidence and this mood of confidence is well expressed in the economy of defensive works. These forts were not strongholds which their garrisons expected to be called upon to defend against siege. They could be held against attack, but such an eventuality would not be commonplace. The defences provided were sufficient to repel the sudden raid, at night or when the garrison was depleted, but were not designed to withstand a prolonged assault. The height of the curtain wall was probably on average only between 5 and 6 m. Gates were simply planned usually with square or rectangular turrets flanking the entrance. Projecting towers, whether at the gates or the angles, were very rare.

Not until the end of the second century is there any evident change in the form of fortifications, and even then change came slowly. Minor changes in the plans of gates and towers begin to be evident from the Antonine period although these changes may have been set in motion somewhat earlier. Some gates were now made to project slightly in front of the curtain-wall and there is a perceptibly greater emphasis upon the importance of angle towers. *Ballistaria*, platforms for spring-guns, occur slightly more frequently. But the over-all tactical scheme evinced by fort defences of about A.D. 200 would have appeared familiar to a soldier of the time of Augustus.

About the middle of the third century, a military order that had long seemed secure began to crumble away. From 238 the Goths repeatedly harassed the lower Danube frontier and won a major success against Roman legionaries in 251. The middle Danube line and the Balkan provinces behind it suffered such disastrous raids from Germanic and nomadic peoples after 250 that by 271 Aurelian decided that Dacia could no longer be held (see above p. 22). The artificial Roman frontier between Rhine and Danube was under great pressure from the Alamanni from the 230s and was finally given up about 260. Not even the great barrier of the Alps could keep back the waves of barbarians as they tried their strength against a weakened and often divided Rome. Most serious of all, from 257 the Franks time and again pierced the frontier on the Rhine and devastated wide areas of the rich provinces of Gaul. In a remarkably brief period, the military initiative had passed from Rome to the barbarian world of northern Europe.

The Roman army of the old pattern was no longer able to deal with the changed situation. When the enemy broke through and ranged widely and unpredictably on Roman soil, as they did with increasing facility, that army was not trained and organized to deal with their rapidly moving bands. New tactics were necessary and so was a new over-all strategic scheme. The Empire of the first and second centuries was like a giant crustacean whose defence lay entirely in its tough external skeleton. Once that outer shield was pierced, the vital organs lay helpless. Forces on the frontiers were no longer enough. If the Empire was to survive, formations of troops were needed within the provinces, equipped to operate in depth behind the frontiers. The emperor Gallienus appears to have taken decisive steps towards the creation of a new and more mobile army with bases at strategic points behind the frontier lines, although in certain frontier regions the advantages of mobility in field forces were grasped as early as the reign of Septimius Severus. These processes, which were to transform the frontier-bound army of the early Empire into the more mobile and flexible force of the fourth century, were accelerated during Gallienus's disturbed reign. But later emperors pursued the policy further, chief among them being Aurelian and Diocletian, until by the time of Constantine I the army consisted of two broad divisions: the field army within the provinces *(comitatenses)* and the less prestigious *limitanei* stationed on the frontiers.

The mode of fortification evident in Aurelian's wall around Rome is thus a product of a time of fundamental change in military organization, in field tactics and in over-all strategy. Until the middle decades of the third century, relatively few cities in the northern and western provinces had been compelled to withstand a siege. Many, indeed, could not have done so, for they were not provided with defences until the late second or third century. In the main, walls were scarcely required at all before the third century and certainly not against external attackers. The danger far more frequently came from within the Empire in the circumstances of native revolts like those raised by

Boudicca and Civilis in the first century, or of intense rivalry between neighbouring cities such as that v hich simmered between Lyon and Vienne. When barbarian armies began to break through into Gaul, Italy and the Balkans during the third century, it seemed inevitable that siege campaigns would play an enlarged role in warfare. In actuality, though sieges did become more frequent, they did not dominate the conduct of war at this time, or indeed later. The principal reason why this was so was that the barbarians now threatening the Empire had no great expertise in siege-warfare, an understandable failing among peoples who had no defended cities of their own. What is more, they were slow to learn the techniques necessary for the building of siege-engines, towers and the like, and even slower to develop the cohesion and deliberation needed to conduct a protracted siege.[31] There were, after all, easier targets for small bands of raiders who appeared inside the frontiers. Rich pickings could be had in the pillaging of open settlements, villas and farmsteads. Almost anything was better than waiting outside the walls of a city until a strong relieving force arrived. It was small wonder that some barbarian leaders gave walled cities a wide berth and reckoned them traps rather than targets. Surprise attacks were certainly a better prospect, but if they failed there was little hope of an investment ending in success for the invaders. By their mere existence, therefore, though they did not guarantee immunity from attack, the provision of defences for cities gave those communities an enormous tactical advantage. Unless the defenders were grossly negligent, their city was unlikely to fall to frontal assault or be brought to its knees by a long blockade.

In order to understand the place of Aurelian's wall in the history of Roman fortification, it is necessary to return to the beginning of the Empire and, in particular, to those features of defences most sensitive to changing tactical theory, gates and towers.

Gates and towers

The gates provided for the new city foundations in Italy and Gaul in the early Empire, and in particular in the reign of Augustus, were first and foremost designed to impress those who passed through them. That cities might have to undergo sieges was an all too bitter memory for many who still remembered the long years of civil strife before 31 B.C.. But the idea that the citizens of these Augustan colonies would need to fight off external enemies would not have been in the forefront of their architects' minds. The gates certainly bear the impress of military planning but they were above all else plain and dignified expressions of the architectural ideals of the day. They impress by their scale and solidity, but still more by their unpretentious combination of the monumental and the functional.

The dominant type of city gate at the beginning of the Empire was one in

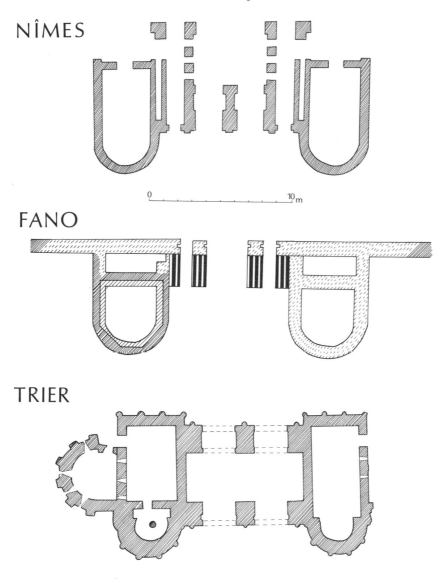

NÎMES

FANO

TRIER

Fig. 35 Plans of early Imperial gates, I:
Nîmes: Augustan
Fano: Augustan
Trier: late second century

which the gate-opening was flanked by projecting towers which might be rectangular, as at Aosta, round-fronted, as at Fano and Nîmes (fig. 35), Arles, Fréjus and Autun, or more rarely polygonal, as at Turin, Spello and Como. The gateway commonly gave access to a rectangular inner courtyard which

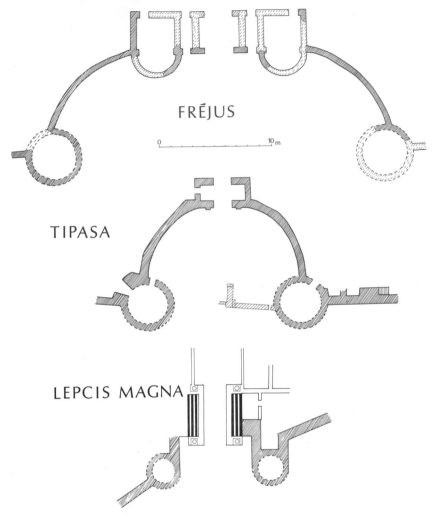

FRÉJUS

TIPASA

LEPCIS MAGNA

Fig. 36 Plans of early Imperial gates, II:
Fréjus: Augustan
Tipasa: second century
Lepcis Magna: third century

might range from the considerable space of the Porta Palatina at Turin to the little court 9·6 m square at Nîmes. The gate with round-fronted towers was to be the longest-lived type and the most widely disseminated. At three cities in southern Gaul, Arles, Aix and Fréjus and at Tipasa in north Africa (fig. 36), the gate houses lay at the back of a large curved forecourt, itself flanked by circular towers projecting from the curtain-wall. The essential features of this type of gate are found in other early Imperial gates in Gaul (e.g. at Toulouse) and are discernible much later in Gallia Belgica (Trier), Germania Inferior (Cologne) and in Britain (Verulamium).

In gates of the later first century A.D. there is an evident tendency towards elaboration on the basic form. At Verona, for example, one of the richest cities in northern Italy at this date, two of the simple Augustan gates were embellished by exuberant baroque façades[32] in a rebuilding after damage caused in the civil strife of A.D. 69. This was no more than rich ornament applied to a gate which in its fundamentals remained unaltered. But at a few cities gates of more elaborate plan than their Augustan forebears were beginning to appear. The east gate of Aventicum (Avenches) in western Switzerland, belonging apparently to the later first century, has a large, circular inner court, like that at Toulouse (fig. 37), and the double portal is

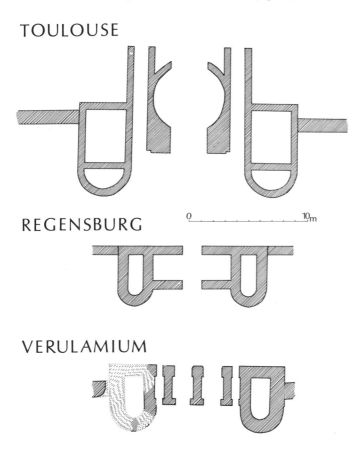

TOULOUSE

REGENSBURG

0 _____ 10m

VERULAMIUM

Fig. 37 Plans of early Imperial gates, III:
Toulouse: Augustan?
Regensburg: A.D. 179
Verulamium: late second century

flanked by massive polygonal towers.[33] There may have been borrowing here from the north Italian tradition, represented for us by the Porta Palatina of Turin, by now a century old.

Very few gates, or indeed entire *enceintes*, are known to date from the first half of the second century: it is not until the later decades of the century that the next group can be distinguished. There has been no profound change in plan, but there is now a more pronounced monumentality. In no gate is this clearer than in the best preserved survivor from this period, the Porta Nigra at Trier (Fig. 35). This most imposing gate possessed two huge and deep flanking towers with semicircular fronts, 20 m long and 9 m wide, originally designed to rise to a height of four stories (about 30 m), and between them an enclosed courtyard measuring 17 m by 8 m and pierced by two passageways. All four stories were decorated front and back with engaged columns, uniform in size in the upper floors, somewhat larger in the ground storey. Both towers and courtyard were lit by frequent and regularly spaced windows in all the stories above the ground floor.

This gate, which surpasses in magnificence all other surviving town gates in the north-western provinces, was never finished, the top storey of the eastern tower not being constructed. The date has been much debated in the past. The most recent survey, and the most thorough yet,[34] produces strong architectural arguments in favour of a date towards the end of the second century, supporting them with the results of excavation carried out in the 1930s and now published for the first time. The Porta Nigra thus seems to occupy a position near to the close of the confident era of imperial fortification. Shortly afterwards, the architecture of gates was to turn in new directions, and it is perhaps appropriate that this ambitious structure was never completed.

By this date the defences and gates of military installations were beginning to change under the influence of civic traditions of building. Projecting towers, both rectangular and round-fronted, began to appear in Antonine forts in Britain, in Germany and in Raetia. A new legionary fortress constructed in the reign of Marcus Aurelius at Castra Regina (Regensburg) (fig. 37) on the upper Danube was equipped with a massive gate of the urban type (its Porta Praetoria), with rather narrow, round-fronted towers flanking a wide gate house.[35] The new feature at Regensburg is the placing of the entire gate structure in front of the curtain-wall, thus emphasizing the function of the gate as a bulwark covering a vulnerable point on the defensive line. Although this gate bears an inscription dating to A.D. 179, it has for long been thought that the surviving structure was the result of a substantial rebuilding of an Antonine gate in the late third century, but now that towers with rounded fronts have been shown to be a relatively common feature of other second-century gates on the upper Danube, the evidence of the inscription can be

LINCOLN

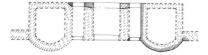

LUGO

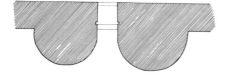

PORTCHESTER

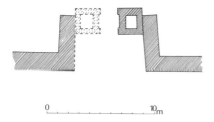

Fig. 38 Plans of third-century gates:
Lincoln, North Gate (Newport Arch)
Lugo, Puerta del Minho
Portchester, Landgate (West Gate)

accepted as giving a true date for the visible structure.

The first half of the third century was a period of increasing diversification in the architecture of gates. The older types, including late versions of the Augustan models, as at Verulamium (fig. 37) and Lincoln (fig. 38) in Britain, were still current but there is now an evident preparedness to meet local needs and exigencies by local expedients, thus producing some highly individual plans. Two examples will illustrate the point. The Porta Oea at Lepcis Magna[36] incorporated in its structure an earlier monumental arch, datable probably to the reign of Hadrian or Antoninus Pius. With scant alteration this monument became the arch over a single carriageway gate, the town wall being carried up to its outer walls without any attempt at bonding (fig. 36).

The arch was set at the base of a small forecourt flanked by two projecting towers. The siting of these means that they were entirely divorced from the main structure and it seems that the architect made no effort to create a structural unit in which the arch and the towers would be effectively combined. The later third century is the most probable context for the Lepcis gate.

Another somewhat awkwardly planned gate is the west gate of the legionary fortress at Vindonissa in Switzerland.[37] This had a single opening with a narrow foot-passage to either side, the whole being guarded by circular towers projecting in asymmetrical fashion to frame a shallow forecourt in front of the gate house. The Vindonissa gate may be plausibly dated to the later third century, probably to a phase of rebuilding after 260. By this date, profound changes were being registered in fortification in most parts of the Empire.

The new fortifications of the late third century

The changes wrought in the defences of towns in the later third century can best be studied in Gaul, the German provinces, Spain and, to a lesser extent, in Britain. The majority of the cities of Gaul which bore the brunt of the barbarian invasions of 253–75 had no defences as far as is known. When the successive waves had spent themselves, an extensive programme of fortification was begun, all the major centres being now defended (or in several cases provided with walled citadels at their heart), along with a large number of lesser settlements and staging-posts along the major roads. The character of these new-style fortifications[38] is well known from surviving examples, among others at Le Mans, Senlis, Carcassonne, Bourges, Périgeux, Bavai, Famars, Beauvais and Soissons. The dominant features in the new mode were broad, high curtain-walls, massive projecting towers, usually sited less than 30 m apart, narrow gate-opening flanked by powerful towers, and, usually, a broad ditch or ditches surrounding the whole work. The massive walls were commonly built on unmortared foundations which consisted largely of re-used masonry, decorative items including columns, sculpture and tombstones being frequently pressed into service. Above this heterogeneous footing the curtain-wall was built in rubble concrete faced with neat cubes of stone, to which the term *petit appareil* is usually applied, and often interspersed with regularly spaced string-courses in brick or tile.

The date of these fortifications is far from well established. The walls of Grenoble (Cularo) alone are dated by inscriptions, in this instance of Diocletian and Maximian, thus giving a date of 286–305. The bridgehead fort at Deutz, facing Cologne across the Rhine, is also firmly dated by a building inscription to 310. It is most probable, however, that the move towards

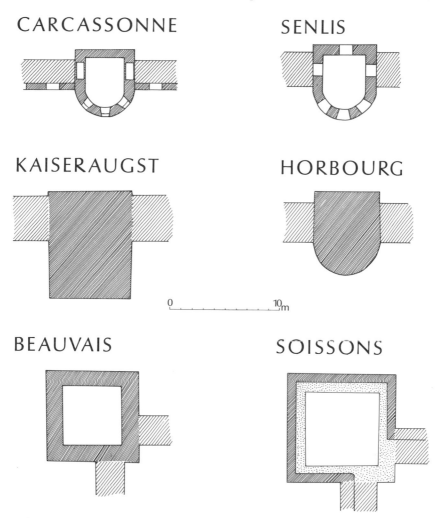

Fig. 39 Towers on late Imperial fortifications, I: Carcassonne, Senlis, Kaiseraugst, Horbourg, Beauvais and Soissons.

massive, towered defences had begun well before the first Tetrarchy. In the tradition recorded by Gregory of Tours, the walls of Dijon are attributed to Aurelian after his recovery of Gaul from the breakaway *Imperium Galliarum* in 274, and other cities may have been fortified in this reign.

From Britain there comes a much stronger indication that the new ideas were being given expression before the time of Diocletian. The foundation of the powerful coastal installations of the Saxon Shore,[39] which are so conspicuous a feature of surviving Roman works in Britain, was given a significant impetus in the later third century, some earlier sites being adapted and remodelled (e.g. Dover, Burgh Castle, Richborough), some new sites chosen (Portchester, Lympne), and at least two earlier forts (Brancaster, Reculver) being retained in the developed scheme. The details of chronology are not clear beyond dispute, but at Richborough the coin evidence strongly suggests that the fort was constructed at latest between 275 and 285. Portchester came a little later (fig. 38), probably between 280 and 290, and perhaps Pevensey too, although the discovery of a coin of 335 beneath one of the towers here has long suggested that this fort was a later addition to the series.

The most striking features of the Gaulish and Spanish fortifications, and in terms of their function the most important, are the projecting towers (fig. 39). Relatively few of the major gates survive, so that direct comparison with those of Aurelianic Rome is not easy or, at least, reliable. There is considerable variety in the plans of towers, but certain traits shared with the fortifications of other western provinces can be discerned. One of the commoner types of tower has a semicircular or horseshoe-shaped front projecting 3 to 5 m in front of the curtain-wall. A number of examples, for instance at Senlis, Beauvais and Yverdon, also project slightly to the rear. These towers were frequently solid to the level of the rampart-walk and probably usually had two chambered stories above, as the towers at Senlis demonstrate. The same tower type is known in military fortifications, for example at Horbourg in Alsace.

Circular, hollow towers lying astride the line of the wall, a type well known in the early Empire, were still occasionally constructed in the later third century but were becoming rare until they were revived in Constantine's reign. Rectangular towers with solid bases, like those of Aurelian's wall, were also common in town defences, but are known in military defences at this date, as at Kaiseraugst, Isny and Richborough. Very large square corner bastions, 6 to 7 m square, were sometimes provided, as at Soissons and Beauvais (fig. 39). Polygonal-fronted towers are one of the most infrequent types at this date, although occasional examples are recorded from the early fourth century and they were to become more prominent as the century wore on.

The presence of fairly large chambers in the surviving towers at the level of the sentry-walk is paralleled on Aurelian's wall and the remains of large openings or casemates in a few towers indicates that, as at Rome itself, the needs of artillery were in the minds of their builders. These casemates are best seen at Senlis but have been recorded elsewhere, in particular at Lugo and Barcelona in Spain, at Boppard on the middle Rhine, and at Pevensey in southern England.

Closest of all of the surviving circuits to that of Rome is a group of city walls in the Spanish provinces.[40] These are distinguished by their very closely

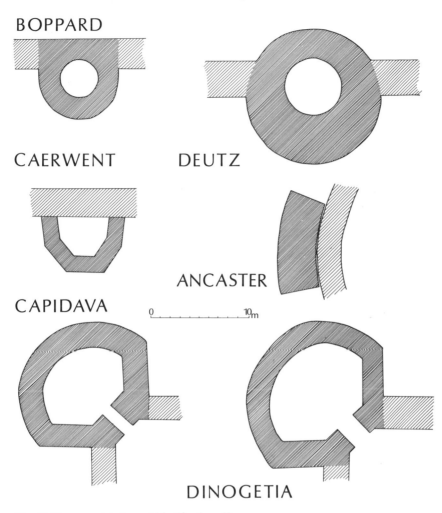

BOPPARD

CAERWENT   DEUTZ

ANCASTER

CAPIDAVA   0 _____ 10m

DINOGETIA

Fig. 40 Towers on late Imperial fortifications, II:
Boppard, Deutz, Caerwent, Ancaster, Capidava and Dinogetia.

set projecting towers, the interval between them being always less than 20 m,
compared with about 30 m on Aurelian's wall. The finest surviving examples
of these fortifications are the city walls of Astorge (Asturica Augusta) and
Lugo (Lucus Augusti), with the legionary fortress of León (Castra Legionis
VII Geminae) close behind. The cities of Barcelona (Barcino) and Zaragoza
(Caesaraugusta) belonged to this group and so, perhaps, did Evora (Ebora).
None of these are closely dated, but the later third century is their probable
context. Nothing quite like these towered circuits is known in Gaul and Italy
and it is thus curious that the closest analogues to the Aurelianic wall, and
roughly contemporary with it, lie 700 to 1,000 km away to the west. There is,

however, no reason to infer that there was any direct link between the Spanish walls and those of Rome. On points of structural detail there is in fact little similarity between them. The Spanish towers, for instance, are generally round-fronted, only those at Barcelona being rectangular, and the gates lack the uniform planning of those in Rome.

It is evident from this brief survey that the later third century was a period of profound change in defensive architecture, and one in which new and old elements mingled together, in some cases in the same circuit. In many respects Aurelian's wall was a product of its time, including both conservative elements and innovations. The simply planned rectangular towers, the galleried sectors, the gates of early Imperial type, all these components owe nothing to the fresh ideas of fortification design at this very date taking concrete form in the western provinces. The conservatism and relative simplicity of the Aurelianic defences may well be due to their construction by the city *collegia*. If they had been built by military engineers, it might be expected that much more of the new modes of fortification would have been manifest in the defences of Rome. That there was not more is due not to conscious archaism, but to men working, against time, in the only tradition known to them. But in one major respect Aurelian's wall was as up to date as it could be. The circuit is among the earliest, if not the earliest, in which the close positioning of the numerous towers and the arrangement of their upper chambers clearly demonstrates the role envisaged for defensive artillery. This in turn strongly suggests that some military intelligence (Aurelian himself, as John Malalas hinted?)[41] had had a say in the planning at the start.

The role *actually* played by artillery in the defence of Rome and other cities in the late Empire is, however, far from clear. The mere fact that there was provision for the machines in Aurelian's wall does not mean that artillery thereafter dominated defensive tactics, as has been assumed by many recent writers on fortifications in the provinces. The increased incidence of sieges from the later third century onward did bring artillery firmly into the plans of those who designed and built city defences. But there is no indication that the importance of artillery was enhanced at this time (quite the contrary),[42] or that the number of units equipped with machines was increased. Each of the mobile field-armies appears to have included at least one legion of artillerymen, but never more than two. In the large area of the Gaulish provinces, for example, there was only one such regiment in the fourth century, though smaller contingents of specially trained troops may also have been assigned to vulnerable sectors of the frontiers. Even this modest provision, however, was probably not made on a permanent basis. It is thus all the more unlikely that *ballistarii* were stationed as a matter of course in cities, even in cities as important as Rome.

Behind its great wall, Rome remained a vigorous and lively place. There has been a tendency among modern writers to assume that after the Gothic success in 410 the city was semi-ruinous, drear and beggarly. There is no justification for that view. The very presence of its strong defences meant that a civilized and prosperous life could go on, and so it did. There are similar signs of an active urbanity at other large Italian cities in the fifth century, at Milan, Aquileia, Verona, Pola, and later at Pavia and Ravenna. All was far from lost and Italy was still a prize to attract Germanic war-lords as a place in which to live and rule. Politically, however, it is true that Rome was now in a backwater. Ravenna now saw more of the Imperial court and in the east there had arisen the New Rome, Constantinople. Throughout the long history of that capital of the eastern Empire, Rome on the Tiber was still encircled by the protective cordon of the wall of Aurelian, Maxentius and Honorius.

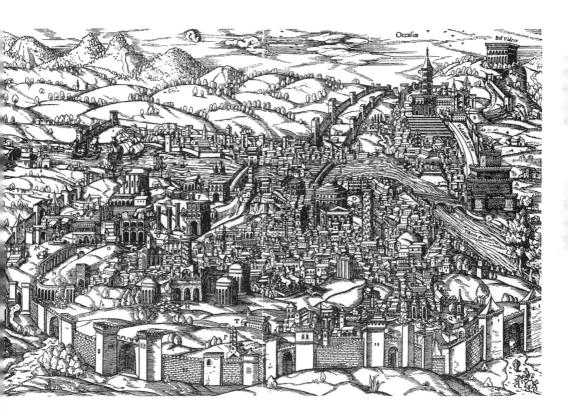

Fig. 41 Rome and her walls in the early sixteenth century. (After a woodcut by Sebastian Münster, Mansell Collection)

The wall today

The visitor to Rome today can examine considerable lengths of the wall. On the north side of the circuit, good stretches of wall, including Porta Pinciana and Porta Nomentana, can be traced through the Pincian gardens and along the Corso d'Italia. This sector ends at the *Castra Praetoria*, where the junction of the wall with the fort may be studied. To the south of *Castra Praetoria* the wall has lost most of its towers. An interesting stretch begins at Porta Tiburtina, extending southwards to where the modern railway breaks through the line of the defences north of Porta Praenestina (now Porta Maggiore). The south side of the city contains the most rewarding sectors of all, especially on a course from *Amphitheatrum Castrense* past Portae Asinaria, Metrobia, Latina, Appia, Ardeatina to Porta Ostiensis East and the Pyramid of Gaius Cestius. Little remains to be seen of the riverside wall and of the fortification west of the Tiber in Trastevere.

References

1 On the beginnings of settlement in the area of Rome: Alföldi 1961, Momigliano 1963, Pallottino 1972 and Ogilvie 1976.
2 Pallottino 1974, esp. 95–7.
3 loc. cit.
4 Livy, I, 36, 1; I, 44, 3. On the *agger*, Varro, *de Ling. Latina* V, 48.
5 Säflund 1932, 44–75.
6 Säflund 1932, Tav. 21 and 23.
7 Säflund 1932, esp. 133–85.
8 Homo 1904 is still useful. The ancient sources are not impressive: Aurelianus in the *Historia Augusta*; Lactantius, *de mortibus persecutorum*; and the later writers Eutropius, Zonaras and Zosimus.
9 Richmond 1927.
10 Richmond 1930, 11; Homo 1904, 262.
11 Notably Syme 1971.
12 Richmond 1930, 12–14.
13 Richmond 1930, 65–6.
14 Richmond 1930, 60.
15 Richmond 1930, 62–3.
16 This important archive of photographs, now deposited in the British Library, has never been published. It is unlikely that reproduction of many of Parker's prints would now be possible.
17 Richmond 1930, 205–17.
18 Richmond 1930, 84–5.
19 John Malalas, *Chron.* xii.
20 *Notizie degli Scavi* 1880, 127–9.
21 Richmond 1930, 224–7.
22 *de Bello Gothico* i, 19.
23 *de Bello Gothico* ii, 9.
24 On the complex history of the fortress, see Richmond 1930, 20–5.
25 *Notizie degli Scavi* 1888, 734; 1889, 17: *Bulletino della Commissione Arch. comunale di Roma* xx (1892), 93.
26 Richmond 1930, 254.
27 Richmond 1930, 254–5.
28 *C.I.L.* vi, 1188 (Porta Portuensis), 1189 (Porta Labicana) and 1190 (Porta Tiburtina).
29 *de Bello Gothico* i, 14–21.
30 There has been no recent, full-scale survey. On gates, Schultze 1909 is frequently referred to but is unreliable as well as out of date. Kähler 1942 is still important, though now needing revision.
31 Thompson 1965, 131–40.
32 *J.R.S.* xxiii (1933), 162–4, Pl. XVIII.2 and Pl. XIX.2; Boethius and Ward-Perkins (1970), 308 and Pl. 166.

33 Stähelin 1948, 604; Schwarz 1964, 23–31.
34 Gose 1969.
35 This gate has never been adequately published. For recent discussion, Bechert 1971, 269–72.
36 *P.B.S.R.* viii (1953), 49–51.
37 Laur-Belart 1935, 32.
38 Butler 1959, von Petrikovits 1971, Johnson 1973.
39 Johnson 1976, esp. 34–62.
40 Richmond 1931.
41 *Chron.* xii.
42 Marsden 1969, 195–8.

Note: these abbreviations are used:
C.I.L.: Corpus Inscriptionum Latinarum
J.R.S.: Journal of Roman Studies
P.B.S.R.: Proceedings of the British School at Rome

Bibliography

Alföldi, A. 1961. *Early Rome and the Latins* (Ann Arbor).

Bechert, T. 1971. Römische Lagertore und ihre Bauinschriften, *Bonner Jahrbücher* clxxi, 201–87.

Boethius, A., and Ward-Perkins, J. B. 1970. *Etruscan and Roman Architecture* (Harmondsworth).

Butler, R. M. 1959. Late Roman town walls in Gaul, *Archaeological Journal* cxvi, 25–50.

Gose, E. 1969. *Der Porta Nigra in Trier* (Berlin).

Homo, L. 1904. *Essai sur le règne de l'empereur Aurelien* (Paris).

Johnson, S. 1973. A group of late Roman City walls in Gallia Belgica, *Britannia* iv, 210–23.

Johnson, S. 1976. *The Roman Forts of the Saxon Shore* (London).

Kähler, H. 1942. Die römischen Torburgen der frühen Kaiserzeit, *Jahrbuch des deutschen archäologischen Instituts* lvii, 1–104.

Laur-Belart, R. 1935. *Vindonissa. Lager und Vicus* (Berlin).

Marsden, E. 1969. *Greek and Roman Artillery. Historical Development* (Oxford).

Momigliano, A. 1963. An interim report on the origins of Rome, *J.R.S.* liii, 95–121.

Nibby, A., and Gell, W. 1821. *Le mura di Roma.*

Ogilvie, R. M. 1976. *Early Rome and the Etruscans* (London).

Pallottino, M. 1972. Le origini di Roma; considerazioni critiche sulle scoperte e sulle discussioni piu recenti, in *Aufstieg und Niedergang der römischen Welt* (ed. H. Temporini) (Berlin and New York) I (1972), 22–47.

Pallottino, M. 1974. *The Etruscans* (London).

Richmond, I. A. 1927. The relation of the Praetorian Camp to Aurelian's Wall of Rome, *P.B.S.R.* x, 12–22.

Richmond, I. A. 1930. *The City Wall of Imperial Rome* (Oxford).

Richmond, I. A. 1931. Five town walls in Hispania Citerior, *J.R.S.* xxi, 86–100.

Richmond, I. A. 1932. Augustan gates at Turin and Spello, *P.B.S.R.* xii, 52–62.

Säflund, G. 1932. *Le mura di Roma repubblicana* (Lund).

Schultze, R. 1909. Die römischen Stadttore, *Bonner Jahrbücher* cxviii, 280–352.

Schwarz, G. T. 1964. *Die Kaiserstadt Aventicum* (Berne and Munich).

Stähelin, F. 1948. *Die Schweiz in römischer Zeit* (Berne).

Syme, R. 1971. *Emperors and Biography. Studies in the Historia Augusta* (Oxford).

Thompson, E. A. 1965. *The Early Germans* (Oxford).

von Petrikovits, H. 1971. Fortifications in the north-western Roman empire from the third to the fifth Centuries A.D., *J.R.S.* lxi, 178–218.

Index